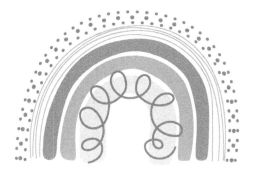

THIS MOOD TRACKER BELONGS TO:

_____

_____

Disclaimer: The information in this book is meant to help track moods and emotions. This tracker should not be used to diagnose or treat any medical conditions.

How to Use This Book

Each page = 1 day. Each day has places to track mood, food, etc twice a day. Use this journal to help identify trends with your moods.

Fill out the prompts

DATE: **8/31/21**   GOAL FOR TODAY: **Be positive!**

MORNING MOOD

HOURS SLEPT: **7**

ENERGY LEVEL:

- VERY HAPPY
- MOSTLY HAPPY
- APATHETIC
- FEELING DOWN
- SAD
- EMOTIONAL
- DISTRESSED/CRYING
- SICK

OTHER EMOTION

HOPELESS   PANIC ATTACK   ISOLATED   LONELY   IRRITATED   ENERGIZED   AGGRESSIVE   ANGER   OTHER:

FOOD: _____

WHAT I THINK PROMPTED THIS MOOD: _____

WHAT ACTION CAN I TAKE FOR THIS MOOD: _____

PHYSICAL ACTIVITY TODAY: **Walked 1 mile**

Circle your moods

AT A GLANCE: MONTHLY MOODS

Choose a color for each mood or emotion. Color in each box with the color of your main mood that day. This can help identify patterns.

☐ HAPPY

☐ SAD

☐ EMOTIONAL

☐ APATHETIC

☐ PANIC ATTACK

☐ ANXIOUS/STRESSED

☐ _ _ _ _ _ _ _ _ _ _

☐ _ _ _ _ _ _ _ _ _ _

☐ _ _ _ _ _ _ _ _ _ _

☐ _ _ _ _ _ _ _ _ _ _

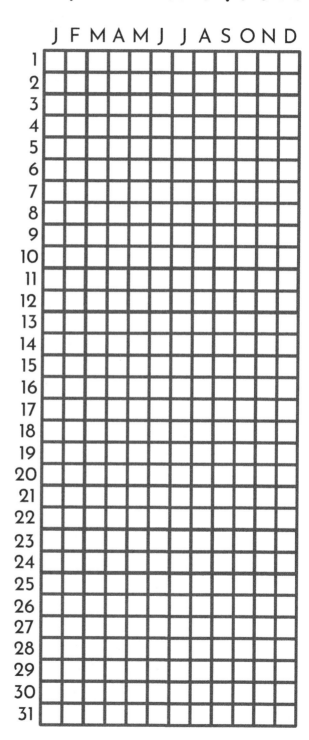

	J	F	M	A	M	J	J	A	S	O	N	D
1												
2												
3												
4												
5												
6												
7												
8												
9												
10												
11												
12												
13												
14												
15												
16												
17												
18												
19												
20												
21												
22												
23												
24												
25												
26												
27												
28												
29												
30												
31												

Date: _____ Goal for today: _____

MORNING MOOD

Hours Slept: 🌙 Energy Level: 🔋

😁 Very happy

🙂 Mostly happy

😐 Apathetic

😞 Feeling down

☹️ Sad

😢 Emotional

😭 Distressed/crying

😷 Sick

Food: _____
_____
_____

What i think prompted this mood: _____
_____
_____

What action can i take for this mood: _____
_____
_____

Physical Activity today: _____
_____

Other Emotions:
Hopeless   Panic attack   Isolated   Lonely   Irritated   Energized   Aggressive   Anger   Other:

• •

EVENING MOOD

Progress towards today's goal: _____

😁 Very happy

🙂 Mostly happy

😐 Apathetic

😞 Feeling down

☹️ Sad

😢 Emotional

😭 Distressed/crying

😷 Sick

Food: _____
_____
_____

What i think prompted this mood: _____
_____
_____

What action can i take for this mood: _____
_____
_____

Something good that happened today: _____

Other Emotions:
Hopeless   Panic attack   Isolated   Lonely   Irritated   Energized   Aggressive   Anger   Other:

Today I am grateful for: _____

Date: _____ Goal for today: _____

MORNING MOOD

Hours Slept: 🌙

Energy Level: 🔋

- 😁 Very happy
- 🙂 Mostly happy
- 😐 Apathetic
- 😔 Feeling down
- 🙁 Sad
- 😢 Emotional
- 😭 Distressed/crying
- 😷 Sick

Food: _____

_____

What i think prompted this mood: _____

_____

_____

What action can i take for this mood: _____

_____

_____

Physical Activity today: _____

_____

Other Emotions:

Hopeless   Panic attack   Isolated   Lonely   Irritated   Energized   Aggressive   Anger   Other:

● ●

EVENING MOOD

Progress towards today's goal: _____

- 😁 Very happy
- 🙂 Mostly happy
- 😐 Apathetic
- 😔 Feeling down
- 🙁 Sad
- 😢 Emotional
- 😭 Distressed/crying
- 😷 Sick

Food: _____

_____

_____

What i think prompted this mood: _____

_____

_____

What action can i take for this mood: _____

_____

_____

Something good that happened today: _____

_____

Other Emotions:

Hopeless   Panic attack   Isolated   Lonely   Irritated   Energized   Aggressive   Anger   Other:

Today I am grateful for: _____

Date: _____ Goal for today: _____

MORNING MOOD

Hours Slept: Energy Level:

😁 Very happy

🙂 Mostly happy

😐 Apathetic

😔 Feeling down

🙁 Sad

😢 Emotional

😭 Distressed/crying

😷 Sick

Other Emotions:
Hopeless   Panic attack   Isolated   Lonely   Irritated   Energized   Aggressive   Anger   Other:

Food: _____
_____
_____

What I think prompted this mood: _____
_____
_____

What action can I take for this mood: _____
_____
_____

Physical Activity today: _____
_____

• •

EVENING MOOD

Progress towards today's goal: _____

😁 Very happy

🙂 Mostly happy

😐 Apathetic

😔 Feeling down

🙁 Sad

😢 Emotional

😭 Distressed/crying

😷 Sick

Other Emotions:
Hopeless   Panic attack   Isolated   Lonely   Irritated   Energized   Aggressive   Anger   Other:

Food: _____
_____
_____

What I think prompted this mood: _____
_____
_____

What action can I take for this mood: _____
_____
_____

Something good that happened today: _____
_____

Today I am grateful for: _____

Date: _____ Goal for today: _____

MORNING MOOD

Hours Slept: 🌙 Energy Level: 🔋

😁 Very happy
🙂 Mostly happy
😐 Apathetic
😔 Feeling down
☹️ Sad
😢 Emotional
😭 Distressed/crying
🤢 sick

Food: _____
_____
_____

What i think prompted this mood: _____
_____
_____

What action can i take for this mood: _____
_____
_____

Physical Activity today: _____
_____

Other Emotions:
Hopeless   Panic attack   Isolated   Lonely   Irritated   Energized   Aggressive   Anger   Other:

• •

EVENING MOOD   Progress towards today's goal: _____

😁 Very happy
🙂 Mostly happy
😐 Apathetic
😔 Feeling down
☹️ Sad
😢 Emotional
😭 Distressed/crying
🤢 sick

Food: _____
_____
_____

What i think prompted this mood: _____
_____
_____

What action can i take for this mood: _____
_____
_____

Something good that happened today: _____
_____

Other Emotions:
Hopeless   Panic attack   Isolated   Lonely   Irritated   Energized   Aggressive   Anger   Other:

Today I am grateful for: _____

Date: _____ Goal for today: _____
_____

MORNING MOOD

Hours Slept: 🌙 Energy Level: 🔋

😁 Very happy

🙂 Mostly happy

😐 Apathetic

😞 Feeling down

🙁 Sad

😢 Emotional

🏠 Distressed/crying

😷 Sick

Food: _____
_____
_____

What i think prompted this mood: _____
_____
_____

What action can i take for this mood: _____
_____
_____

Physical Activity today: _____
_____

Other Emotions:
Hopeless   Panic attack   Isolated   Lonely   Irritated   Energized   Aggressive   Anger   Other:

- -

EVENING MOOD

Progress towards today's goal: _____

😁 Very happy

🙂 Mostly happy

😐 Apathetic

😞 Feeling down

🙁 Sad

😢 Emotional

🏠 Distressed/crying

😷 Sick

Food: _____
_____
_____

What i think prompted this mood: _____
_____
_____

What action can i take for this mood: _____
_____
_____

Something good that happened today: _____
_____

Other Emotions:
Hopeless   Panic attack   Isolated   Lonely   Irritated   Energized   Aggressive   Anger   Other:

Today I am grateful for: _____

Date: _____ Goal for today: _____

MORNING MOOD

Hours Slept: 🌙

Energy Level: 🔋

- 😁 Very happy
- 🙂 Mostly happy
- 😐 Apathetic
- 😔 Feeling down
- 🙁 Sad
- 😢 Emotional
- 🏠 Distressed/crying
- 😷 Sick

Food: _____
_____
_____

What i think prompted this mood: _____
_____
_____

What action can i take for this mood: _____
_____
_____

Physical Activity today: _____
_____

Other Emotions:

Hopeless   Panic attack   Isolated   Lonely   Irritated   Energized   Aggressive   Anger   Other:

· ·

EVENING MOOD

Progress towards today's goal: _____

- 😁 Very happy
- 🙂 Mostly happy
- 😐 Apathetic
- 😔 Feeling down
- 🙁 Sad
- 😢 Emotional
- 🏠 Distressed/crying
- 😷 Sick

Food: _____
_____
_____

What i think prompted this mood: _____
_____
_____

What action can i take for this mood: _____
_____
_____

Something good that happened today: _____
_____

Other Emotions:

Hopeless   Panic attack   Isolated   Lonely   Irritated   Energized   Aggressive   Anger   Other:

Today I am grateful for: _____

Date: _____ Goal for today: _____

MORNING MOOD

Hours Slept:

Energy Level:

- 😄 Very happy
- 🙂 Mostly happy
- 😐 Apathetic
- 😞 Feeling down
- 🙁 Sad
- 😢 Emotional
- 😭 Distressed/crying
- 😷 Sick

Food: _____
_____

What i think prompted this mood: _____
_____

What action can i take for this mood: _____
_____

Physical Activity today: _____
_____

Other Emotions:
Hopeless Panic attack Isolated Lonely Irritated Energized Aggressive Anger Other:

• •

EVENING MOOD

Progress towards today's goal: _____

- 😄 Very happy
- 🙂 Mostly happy
- 😐 Apathetic
- 😞 Feeling down
- 🙁 Sad
- 😢 Emotional
- 😭 Distressed/crying
- 😷 Sick

Food: _____
_____

What i think prompted this mood: _____
_____

What action can i take for this mood: _____
_____

Something good that happened today: _____
_____

Other Emotions:
Hopeless Panic attack Isolated Lonely Irritated Energized Aggressive Anger Other:

Today I am grateful for: _____

Date: _____ Goal for today: _____

MORNING MOOD

Hours Slept:

Energy Level:

- 😁 Very happy
- 🙂 Mostly happy
- 😐 Apathetic
- 😔 Feeling down
- 🙁 Sad
- 😢 Emotional
- 😭 Distressed/crying
- 😷 Sick

Food: _____
_____
_____

What i think prompted this mood: _____
_____
_____

What action can i take for this mood: _____
_____
_____

Physical Activity today: _____
_____

Other Emotions:
Hopeless   Panic attack   Isolated   Lonely   Irritated   Energized   Aggressive   Anger   Other:

• •

EVENING MOOD

Progress towards today's goal: _____

- 😁 Very happy
- 🙂 Mostly happy
- 😐 Apathetic
- 😔 Feeling down
- 🙁 Sad
- 😢 Emotional
- 😭 Distressed/crying
- 😷 Sick

Food: _____
_____
_____

What i think prompted this mood: _____
_____
_____

What action can i take for this mood: _____
_____
_____

Something good that happened today: _____
_____

Other Emotions:
Hopeless   Panic attack   Isolated   Lonely   Irritated   Energized   Aggressive   Anger   Other:

Today I am grateful for: _____

Date: _____ Goal for today: _____

MORNING MOOD

Hours Slept:

Energy Level:

😁 Very happy

🙂 Mostly happy

😐 Apathetic

😔 Feeling down

🙁 Sad

😢 Emotional

😭 Distressed/crying

😷 sick

Food: _____
_____
_____

What i think prompted this mood: _____
_____
_____

What action can i take for this mood: _____
_____
_____

Physical Activity today: _____
_____

Other Emotions:
Hopeless   Panic attack   Isolated   Lonely   Irritated   Energized   Aggressive   Anger   Other:

• •

EVENING MOOD

Progress towards today's goal: _____

😁 Very happy

🙂 Mostly happy

😐 Apathetic

😔 Feeling down

🙁 Sad

😢 Emotional

😭 Distressed/crying

😷 sick

Food: _____
_____

What i think prompted this mood: _____
_____
_____

What action can i take for this mood: _____
_____
_____

Something good that happened today: _____
_____

Other Emotions:
Hopeless   Panic attack   Isolated   Lonely   Irritated   Energized   Aggressive   Anger   Other:

Today I am grateful for: _____

Date: _____ Goal for today: _____

MORNING MOOD

Hours Slept:

Energy Level:

😁 Very happy

🙂 Mostly happy

😐 Apathetic

😞 Feeling down

🙁 Sad

😢 Emotional

😭 Distressed/crying

🤢 Sick

Food: _____
_____
_____

What i think prompted this mood: _____
_____
_____

What action can i take for this mood: _____
_____
_____

Physical Activity today: _____
_____

Other Emotions:
Hopeless   Panic attack   Isolated   Lonely   Irritated   Energized   Aggressive   Anger   Other:

• •

EVENING MOOD

Progress towards today's goal: _____

😁 Very happy

🙂 Mostly happy

😐 Apathetic

😞 Feeling down

🙁 Sad

😢 Emotional

😭 Distressed/crying

🤢 Sick

Food: _____
_____
_____

What i think prompted this mood: _____
_____
_____

What action can i take for this mood: _____
_____
_____

Something good that happened today: _____
_____

Other Emotions:
Hopeless   Panic attack   Isolated   Lonely   Irritated   Energized   Aggressive   Anger   Other:

Today I am grateful for: _____

Date: _____ Goal for today: _____

MORNING MOOD

Hours Slept:

Energy Level:

😁 Very happy

🙂 Mostly happy

😐 Apathetic

😣 Feeling down

☹️ Sad

😢 Emotional

😭 Distressed/crying

🤢 Sick

Food: _____
_____
_____

What i think prompted this mood: _____
_____
_____

What action can i take for this mood: _____
_____
_____

Physical Activity today: _____
_____

Other Emotions:
Hopeless   Panic attack   Isolated   Lonely   Irritated   Energized   Aggressive   Anger   Other:

- -

EVENING MOOD

Progress towards today's goal: _____

😁 Very happy

🙂 Mostly happy

😐 Apathetic

😣 Feeling down

☹️ Sad

😢 Emotional

😭 Distressed/crying

🤢 Sick

Food: _____
_____
_____

What i think prompted this mood: _____
_____
_____

What action can i take for this mood: _____
_____
_____

Something good that happened today: _____
_____

Other Emotions:
Hopeless   Panic attack   Isolated   Lonely   Irritated   Energized   Aggressive   Anger   Other:

Today I am grateful for: _____

Date: _____   Goal for today: _____

MORNING MOOD

Hours Slept: 🌙   Energy Level: 🔋

😁 Very happy
🙂 Mostly happy
😐 Apathetic
😔 Feeling down
🙁 Sad
😢 Emotional
😭 Distressed/crying
😷 Sick

Food: _____
_____
_____

What I think prompted this mood: _____
_____
_____

What action can I take for this mood: _____
_____
_____

Physical Activity today: _____
_____

Other Emotions:
Hopeless   Panic attack   Isolated   Lonely   Irritated   Energized   Aggressive   Anger   Other:

• •

EVENING MOOD

Progress towards today's goal: _____

😁 Very happy
🙂 Mostly happy
😐 Apathetic
😔 Feeling down
🙁 Sad
😢 Emotional
😭 Distressed/crying
😷 Sick

Food: _____
_____
_____

What I think prompted this mood: _____
_____
_____

What action can I take for this mood: _____
_____
_____

Something good that happened today: _____
_____

Other Emotions:
Hopeless   Panic attack   Isolated   Lonely   Irritated   Energized   Aggressive   Anger   Other:

Today I am grateful for: _____

Date: _____ Goal for today: _____

MORNING MOOD

Hours Slept:

Energy Level:

- 😁 Very happy
- 🙂 Mostly happy
- 😐 Apathetic
- 😔 Feeling down
- ☹️ Sad
- 😢 Emotional
- 😭 Distressed/crying
- 😷 sick

Food: _____
_____
_____

What i think prompted this mood: _____
_____
_____

What action can i take for this mood: _____
_____
_____

Physical Activity today: _____
_____

Other Emotions:
Hopeless   Panic attack   Isolated   Lonely   Irritated   Energized   Aggressive   Anger   Other:

EVENING MOOD

Progress towards today's goal: _____

- 😁 Very happy
- 🙂 Mostly happy
- 😐 Apathetic
- 😔 Feeling down
- ☹️ Sad
- 😢 Emotional
- 😭 Distressed/crying
- 😷 sick

Food: _____
_____
_____

What i think prompted this mood: _____
_____
_____

What action can i take for this mood: _____
_____
_____

Something good that happened today: _____
_____

Other Emotions:
Hopeless   Panic attack   Isolated   Lonely   Irritated   Energized   Aggressive   Anger   Other:

Today I am grateful for: _____

Date: _____   Goal for today: _____

MORNING MOOD

Hours Slept: 🌙

Energy Level: 🔋

😁 Very happy

🙂 Mostly happy

😐 Apathetic

😞 Feeling down

🙁 Sad

😢 Emotional

😭 Distressed/crying

🤢 Sick

Food: _____
_____
_____

What I think prompted this mood: _____
_____
_____

What action can I take for this mood: _____
_____
_____

Physical Activity today: _____
_____

Other Emotions:
Hopeless   Panic attack   Isolated   Lonely   Irritated   Energized   Aggressive   Anger   Other:

• •

EVENING MOOD

Progress towards today's goal: _____

😁 Very happy

🙂 Mostly happy

😐 Apathetic

😞 Feeling down

🙁 Sad

😢 Emotional

😭 Distressed/crying

🤢 Sick

Food: _____
_____
_____

What I think prompted this mood: _____
_____
_____

What action can I take for this mood: _____
_____

Something good that happened today: _____
_____

Other Emotions:
Hopeless   Panic attack   Isolated   Lonely   Irritated   Energized   Aggressive   Anger   Other:

Today I am grateful for: _____

Date: _____ Goal for today: _____

MORNING MOOD

Hours Slept: 🌙

Energy Level: 🔋

- 😄 Very happy
- 🙂 Mostly happy
- 😐 Apathetic
- 😞 Feeling down
- ☹️ Sad
- 😢 Emotional
- 😭 Distressed/crying
- 😷 Sick

Food: _____
_____
_____

What i think prompted this mood: _____
_____
_____

What action can i take for this mood: _____
_____
_____

Physical Activity today: _____
_____

Other Emotions:
Hopeless   Panic attack   Isolated   Lonely   Irritated   Energized   Aggressive   Anger   Other:

· ·

EVENING MOOD

Progress towards today's goal: _____

- 😄 Very happy
- 🙂 Mostly happy
- 😐 Apathetic
- 😞 Feeling down
- ☹️ Sad
- 😢 Emotional
- 😭 Distressed/crying
- 😷 Sick

Food: _____
_____
_____

What i think prompted this mood: _____
_____
_____

What action can i take for this mood: _____
_____
_____

Something good that happened today: _____
_____

Other Emotions:
Hopeless   Panic attack   Isolated   Lonely   Irritated   Energized   Aggressive   Anger   Other:

Today I am grateful for: _____

Date: _____   Goal for today: _____

MORNING MOOD

Hours Slept: 🌙

Energy Level: 🔋

😁 Very happy

🙂 Mostly happy

😐 Apathetic

😔 Feeling down

🙁 Sad

😢 Emotional

🏠 Distressed/crying

😷 Sick

Food: _____
_____
_____

What I think prompted this mood: _____
_____
_____

What action can I take for this mood: _____
_____
_____

Physical Activity today: _____
_____

Other Emotions:
Hopeless   Panic attack   Isolated   Lonely   Irritated   Energized   Aggressive   Anger   Other:

• •

EVENING MOOD

Progress towards today's goal: _____

😁 Very happy

🙂 Mostly happy

😐 Apathetic

😔 Feeling down

🙁 Sad

😢 Emotional

🏠 Distressed/crying

😷 Sick

Food: _____
_____
_____

What I think prompted this mood: _____
_____
_____

What action can I take for this mood: _____
_____
_____

Something good that happened today: _____
_____

Other Emotions:
Hopeless   Panic attack   Isolated   Lonely   Irritated   Energized   Aggressive   Anger   Other:

Today I am grateful for: _____

Date: _____ Goal for today: _____

MORNING MOOD

Hours Slept: 🌙

Energy Level: 🔋

😁 Very happy
🙂 Mostly happy
😐 Apathetic
😔 Feeling down
☹️ Sad
😢 Emotional
🏠 Distressed/crying
😷 Sick

Food: _____
_____
_____

What I think prompted this mood: _____
_____
_____

What action can I take for this mood: _____
_____
_____

Physical Activity today: _____
_____

Other Emotions:
Hopeless   Panic attack   Isolated   Lonely   Irritated   Energized   Aggressive   Anger   Other:

•••

EVENING MOOD

Progress towards today's goal: _____

😁 Very happy
🙂 Mostly happy
😐 Apathetic
😔 Feeling down
☹️ Sad
😢 Emotional
🏠 Distressed/crying
😷 Sick

Food: _____
_____
_____

What I think prompted this mood: _____
_____
_____

What action can I take for this mood: _____
_____
_____

Something good that happened today: _____
_____

Other Emotions:
Hopeless   Panic attack   Isolated   Lonely   Irritated   Energized   Aggressive   Anger   Other:

Today I am grateful for: _____

Date: _____ GOAL FOR TODAY: _____

MORNING MOOD

HOURS SLEPT: 🌙   ENERGY LEVEL: 🔋

😁 VERY HAPPY

🙂 MOSTLY HAPPY

😐 APATHETIC

😔 FEELING DOWN

☹️ SAD

😢 EMOTIONAL

😭 DISTRESSED/CRYING

😷 SICK

FOOD: _____
_____
_____

WHAT I THINK PROMPTED THIS MOOD: _____
_____
_____

WHAT ACTION CAN I TAKE FOR THIS MOOD: _____
_____
_____

PHYSICAL ACTIVITY TODAY: _____
_____

OTHER EMOTIONS:
HOPELESS   PANIC ATTACK   ISOLATED   LONELY   IRRITATED   ENERGIZED   AGGRESSIVE   ANGER   OTHER:

· ·

EVENING MOOD

PROGRESS TOWARDS TODAY'S GOAL: _____

😁 VERY HAPPY

🙂 MOSTLY HAPPY

😐 APATHETIC

😔 FEELING DOWN

☹️ SAD

😢 EMOTIONAL

😭 DISTRESSED/CRYING

😷 SICK

FOOD: _____
_____
_____

WHAT I THINK PROMPTED THIS MOOD: _____
_____
_____

WHAT ACTION CAN I TAKE FOR THIS MOOD: _____
_____

SOMETHING GOOD THAT HAPPENED TODAY: _____
_____

OTHER EMOTIONS:
HOPELESS   PANIC ATTACK   ISOLATED   LONELY   IRRITATED   ENERGIZED   AGGRESSIVE   ANGER   OTHER:

TODAY I AM GRATEFUL FOR: _____

Date: _____ Goal for today: _____

MORNING MOOD

Hours Slept: 🌙   Energy Level: 🔋

😁 Very happy

🙂 Mostly happy

😐 Apathetic

😔 Feeling down

🙁 Sad

😢 Emotional

🏠 Distressed/crying

😷 Sick

Food: _____
_____
_____

What i think prompted this mood: _____
_____
_____

What action can i take for this mood: _____
_____
_____

Physical Activity today: _____
_____

Other Emotions:
Hopeless   Panic attack   Isolated   Lonely   Irritated   Energized   Aggressive   Anger   Other:

• •

EVENING MOOD

Progress towards today's goal: _____

😁 Very happy

🙂 Mostly happy

😐 Apathetic

😔 Feeling down

🙁 Sad

😢 Emotional

🏠 Distressed/crying

😷 Sick

Food: _____
_____
_____

What i think prompted this mood: _____
_____
_____

What action can i take for this mood: _____
_____
_____

Something good that happened today: _____
_____

Other Emotions:
Hopeless   Panic attack   Isolated   Lonely   Irritated   Energized   Aggressive   Anger   Other:

Today I am grateful for: _____

DATE: _____   GOAL FOR TODAY: _____

MORNING MOOD

HOURS SLEPT: ENERGY LEVEL:

- 😁 VERY HAPPY
- 🙂 MOSTLY HAPPY
- 😐 APATHETIC
- 😔 FEELING DOWN
- ☹️ SAD
- 😢 EMOTIONAL
- 🏠 DISTRESSED/CRYING
- 😷 SICK

FOOD: _____
_____

WHAT I THINK PROMPTED THIS MOOD: _____
_____
_____

WHAT ACTION CAN I TAKE FOR THIS MOOD: _____
_____
_____

PHYSICAL ACTIVITY TODAY: _____
_____

OTHER EMOTIONS:
HOPELESS   PANIC ATTACK   ISOLATED   LONELY   IRRITATED   ENERGIZED   AGGRESSIVE   ANGER   OTHER:

• •

EVENING MOOD

PROGRESS TOWARDS TODAY'S GOAL: _____

- 😁 VERY HAPPY
- 🙂 MOSTLY HAPPY
- 😐 APATHETIC
- 😔 FEELING DOWN
- ☹️ SAD
- 😢 EMOTIONAL
- 🏠 DISTRESSED/CRYING
- 😷 SICK

FOOD: _____
_____
_____

WHAT I THINK PROMPTED THIS MOOD: _____
_____
_____

WHAT ACTION CAN I TAKE FOR THIS MOOD: _____
_____
_____

SOMETHING GOOD THAT HAPPENED TODAY: _____

OTHER EMOTIONS:
HOPELESS   PANIC ATTACK   ISOLATED   LONELY   IRRITATED   ENERGIZED   AGGRESSIVE   ANGER   OTHER:

TODAY I AM GRATEFUL FOR: _____

Date: _____ GOAL FOR TODAY: _____

MORNING MOOD

HOURS SLEPT: 🌙

ENERGY LEVEL: 🔋

😁 VERY HAPPY

🙂 MOSTLY HAPPY

😐 APATHETIC

😔 FEELING DOWN

🙁 SAD

😢 EMOTIONAL

😭 DISTRESSED/CRYING

😷 SICK

FOOD: _____
_____
_____

WHAT I THINK PROMPTED THIS MOOD: _____
_____
_____

WHAT ACTION CAN I TAKE FOR THIS MOOD: _____
_____
_____

PHYSICAL ACTIVITY TODAY: _____
_____

Other Emotions:
Hopeless   Panic attack   Isolated   Lonely   Irritated   Energized   Aggressive   Anger   Other:

• •

EVENING MOOD

PROGRESS TOWARDS TODAY'S GOAL: _____

😁 VERY HAPPY

🙂 MOSTLY HAPPY

😐 APATHETIC

😔 FEELING DOWN

🙁 SAD

😢 EMOTIONAL

😭 DISTRESSED/CRYING

😷 SICK

FOOD: _____
_____
_____

WHAT I THINK PROMPTED THIS MOOD: _____
_____

WHAT ACTION CAN I TAKE FOR THIS MOOD: _____
_____

SOMETHING GOOD THAT HAPPENED TODAY: _____
_____

Other Emotions:
Hopeless   Panic attack   Isolated   Lonely   Irritated   Energized   Aggressive   Anger   Other:

TODAY I AM GRATEFUL FOR: _____

Date: _____ Goal for today: _____

MORNING MOOD

Hours Slept: 🌙 Energy Level: 🔋

😁 Very happy

🙂 Mostly happy

😐 Apathetic

😔 Feeling down

☹️ Sad

😢 Emotional

🏠 Distressed/crying

😷 Sick

Food: _____
_____
_____

What i think prompted this mood: _____
_____
_____

What action can i take for this mood: _____
_____
_____

Physical Activity today: _____
_____

Other Emotions:
Hopeless   Panic attack   Isolated   Lonely   Irritated   Energized   Aggressive   Anger   Other:

• •

EVENING MOOD

Progress towards today's goal: _____

😁 Very happy

🙂 Mostly happy

😐 Apathetic

😔 Feeling down

☹️ Sad

😢 Emotional

🏠 Distressed/crying

😷 Sick

Food: _____
_____
_____

What i think prompted this mood: _____
_____
_____

What action can i take for this mood: _____
_____
_____

Something good that happened today: _____
_____

Other Emotions:
Hopeless   Panic attack   Isolated   Lonely   Irritated   Energized   Aggressive   Anger   Other:

Today I am grateful for: _____

Date: _____ Goal for today: _____

MORNING MOOD

Hours
Slept:

Energy
Level:

- 😄 Very happy
- 🙂 Mostly happy
- 😐 Apathetic
- 😞 Feeling down
- 😢 Sad
- 😢 Emotional
- 😭 Distressed/crying
- 😷 Sick

Food: _____
_____
_____

What i think prompted this mood: _____
_____
_____

What action can i take for this mood: _____
_____
_____

Physical Activity today: _____
_____

Other Emotions:
Hopeless   Panic attack   Isolated   Lonely   Irritated   Energized   Aggressive   Anger   Other:

EVENING MOOD

Progress towards today's goal: _____

- 😄 Very happy
- 🙂 Mostly happy
- 😐 Apathetic
- 😞 Feeling down
- 😢 Sad
- 😢 Emotional
- 😭 Distressed/crying
- 😷 Sick

Food: _____
_____
_____

What i think prompted this mood: _____
_____
_____

What action can i take for this mood: _____
_____
_____

Something good that happened today: _____
_____

Other Emotions:
Hopeless   Panic attack   Isolated   Lonely   Irritated   Energized   Aggressive   Anger   Other:

Today I am grateful for: _____

Date: _____ Goal for today: _____

MORNING MOOD

Hours Slept: 🌙

Energy Level: 🔋

😁	Very happy
🙂	Mostly happy
😐	Apathetic
😞	Feeling down
🙁	Sad
😢	Emotional
😭	Distressed/crying
🤢	Sick

Food: _____
_____
_____

What I think prompted this mood: _____
_____
_____

What action can I take for this mood: _____
_____
_____

Physical Activity today: _____
_____

Other Emotions:

Hopeless   Panic attack   Isolated   Lonely   Irritated   Energized   Aggressive   Anger   Other:

• •

EVENING MOOD

Progress towards today's goal: _____

😁	Very happy
🙂	Mostly happy
😐	Apathetic
😞	Feeling down
🙁	Sad
😢	Emotional
😭	Distressed/crying
🤢	Sick

Food: _____
_____
_____

What I think prompted this mood: _____
_____
_____

What action can I take for this mood: _____
_____

Something good that happened today: _____
_____

Other Emotions:

Hopeless   Panic attack   Isolated   Lonely   Irritated   Energized   Aggressive   Anger   Other:

Today I am grateful for: _____

Date: _____ Goal for today: _____

MORNING MOOD

Hours Slept: 🌙

Energy Level: 🔋

😁 Very happy

😊 Mostly happy

😐 Apathetic

😣 Feeling down

🙁 Sad

😢 Emotional

🏠 Distressed/crying

😖 Sick

Food: _____
_____
_____

What i think prompted this mood: _____
_____
_____

What action can i take for this mood: _____
_____
_____

Physical Activity today: _____
_____

Other Emotions:
Hopeless   Panic attack   Isolated   Lonely   Irritated   Energized   Aggressive   Anger   Other:

. . . .

EVENING MOOD

Progress towards today's goal: _____

😁 Very happy

😊 Mostly happy

😐 Apathetic

😣 Feeling down

🙁 Sad

😢 Emotional

🏠 Distressed/crying

😖 Sick

Food: _____
_____
_____

What i think prompted this mood: _____
_____
_____

What action can i take for this mood: _____
_____
_____

Something good that happened today: _____
_____

Other Emotions:
Hopeless   Panic attack   Isolated   Lonely   Irritated   Energized   Aggressive   Anger   Other:

Today I am grateful for: _____

Date: _____ Goal for today: _____

MORNING MOOD

Hours Slept: 🌙

Energy Level: 🔋

😁 Very happy

🙂 Mostly happy

😐 Apathetic

😔 Feeling down

🙁 Sad

😢 Emotional

😭 Distressed/crying

🤢 Sick

Food: _____
_____
_____

What i think prompted this mood: _____
_____
_____

What action can i take for this mood: _____
_____
_____

Physical Activity today: _____
_____

Other Emotions:

Hopeless   Panic attack   Isolated   Lonely   Irritated   Energized   Aggressive   Anger   Other:

● ●

EVENING MOOD

Progress towards today's goal: _____

😁 Very happy

🙂 Mostly happy

😐 Apathetic

😔 Feeling down

🙁 Sad

😢 Emotional

😭 Distressed/crying

🤢 Sick

Food: _____
_____
_____

What i think prompted this mood: _____
_____
_____

What action can i take for this mood: _____
_____
_____

Something good that happened today: _____
_____

Other Emotions:

Hopeless   Panic attack   Isolated   Lonely   Irritated   Energized   Aggressive   Anger   Other:

Today I am grateful for: _____

Date: _____ Goal for today: _____

MORNING MOOD

Hours Slept: 🌙

Energy Level: 🔋

😁 Very happy

🙂 Mostly happy

😐 Apathetic

😔 Feeling down

☹️ Sad

😢 Emotional

😭 Distressed/crying

🤢 Sick

Food: _____
_____
_____

What i think prompted this mood: _____
_____
_____

What action can i take for this mood: _____
_____
_____

Physical Activity today: _____
_____

Other Emotions:
Hopeless   Panic attack   Isolated   Lonely   Irritated   Energized   Aggressive   Anger   Other:

• •

EVENING MOOD

Progress towards today's goal: _____

😁 Very happy

🙂 Mostly happy

😐 Apathetic

😔 Feeling down

☹️ Sad

😢 Emotional

😭 Distressed/crying

🤢 Sick

Food: _____
_____
_____

What i think prompted this mood: _____
_____
_____

What action can i take for this mood: _____
_____
_____

Something good that happened today: _____
_____

Other Emotions:
Hopeless   Panic attack   Isolated   Lonely   Irritated   Energized   Aggressive   Anger   Other:

Today I am grateful for: _____

Date: _____ Goal for today: _____

MORNING MOOD

Hours Slept: 🌙

Energy Level: 🔋

- 😁 Very happy
- 🙂 Mostly happy
- 😐 Apathetic
- 😔 Feeling down
- 🙁 Sad
- 😢 Emotional
- 😭 Distressed/crying
- 😷 Sick

Food: _____
_____
_____

What I think prompted this mood: _____
_____
_____

What action can I take for this mood: _____
_____
_____

Physical Activity today: _____
_____

Other Emotions:
Hopeless   Panic attack   Isolated   Lonely   Irritated   Energized   Aggressive   Anger   Other:

• •

EVENING MOOD

Progress towards today's goal: _____

- 😁 Very happy
- 🙂 Mostly happy
- 😐 Apathetic
- 😔 Feeling down
- 🙁 Sad
- 😢 Emotional
- 😭 Distressed/crying
- 😷 Sick

Food: _____
_____
_____

What I think prompted this mood: _____
_____
_____

What action can I take for this mood: _____
_____
_____

Something good that happened today: _____
_____

Other Emotions:
Hopeless   Panic attack   Isolated   Lonely   Irritated   Energized   Aggressive   Anger   Other:

Today I am grateful for: _____

Date: _____ Goal for today: _____

MORNING MOOD

Hours Slept:

Energy Level:

😁 Very happy

🙂 Mostly happy

😐 Apathetic

😔 Feeling down

☹️ Sad

😢 Emotional

😭 Distressed/crying

😣 Sick

Food: _____
_____
_____

What I think prompted this mood: _____
_____
_____

What action can I take for this mood: _____
_____
_____

Physical Activity today: _____
_____

Other Emotions:
Hopeless   Panic attack   Isolated   Lonely   Irritated   Energized   Aggressive   Anger   Other:

EVENING MOOD

Progress towards today's goal: _____

😁 Very happy

🙂 Mostly happy

😐 Apathetic

😔 Feeling down

☹️ Sad

😢 Emotional

😭 Distressed/crying

😣 Sick

Food: _____
_____
_____

What I think prompted this mood: _____
_____
_____

What action can I take for this mood: _____
_____
_____

Something good that happened today: _____
_____

Other Emotions:
Hopeless   Panic attack   Isolated   Lonely   Irritated   Energized   Aggressive   Anger   Other:

Today I am grateful for: _____

DATE: _____ GOAL FOR TODAY: _____

MORNING MOOD

HOURS SLEPT: 🌙

ENERGY LEVEL: 🔋

😁 VERY HAPPY
🙂 MOSTLY HAPPY
😐 APATHETIC
😔 FEELING DOWN
🙁 SAD
😢 EMOTIONAL
🏚 DISTRESSED/CRYING
😷 SICK

FOOD: _____
_____
_____

WHAT I THINK PROMPTED THIS MOOD: _____
_____
_____

WHAT ACTION CAN I TAKE FOR THIS MOOD: _____
_____
_____

PHYSICAL ACTIVITY TODAY: _____
_____

OTHER EMOTIONS:
HOPELESS   PANIC ATTACK   ISOLATED   LONELY   IRRITATED   ENERGIZED   AGGRESSIVE   ANGER   OTHER:

• •

EVENING MOOD

PROGRESS TOWARDS TODAY'S GOAL: _____

😁 VERY HAPPY
🙂 MOSTLY HAPPY
😐 APATHETIC
😔 FEELING DOWN
🙁 SAD
😢 EMOTIONAL
🏚 DISTRESSED/CRYING
😷 SICK

FOOD: _____
_____

WHAT I THINK PROMPTED THIS MOOD: _____
_____
_____

WHAT ACTION CAN I TAKE FOR THIS MOOD: _____
_____
_____

SOMETHING GOOD THAT HAPPENED TODAY: _____
_____

OTHER EMOTIONS:
HOPELESS   PANIC ATTACK   ISOLATED   LONELY   IRRITATED   ENERGIZED   AGGRESSIVE   ANGER   OTHER:

TODAY I AM GRATEFUL FOR: _____

Date: _____ Goal for today: _____

MORNING MOOD

Hours Slept:

Energy Level:

😄 Very happy

🙂 Mostly happy

😐 Apathetic

😥 Feeling down

☹️ Sad

😢 Emotional

😭 Distressed/crying

😷 Sick

Food: _____
_____
_____

What i think prompted this mood: _____
_____
_____

What action can i take for this mood: _____
_____
_____

Physical Activity today: _____
_____

Other Emotions:

Hopeless   Panic attack   Isolated   Lonely   Irritated   Energized   Aggressive   Anger   Other:

EVENING MOOD

Progress towards today's goal: _____

😄 Very happy

🙂 Mostly happy

😐 Apathetic

😥 Feeling down

☹️ Sad

😢 Emotional

😭 Distressed/crying

😷 Sick

Food: _____
_____
_____

What i think prompted this mood: _____
_____
_____

What action can i take for this mood: _____
_____
_____

Something good that happened today: _____
_____

Other Emotions:

Hopeless   Panic attack   Isolated   Lonely   Irritated   Energized   Aggressive   Anger   Other:

Today I am grateful for: _____

Date: _____   Goal for today: _____

MORNING MOOD

Hours Slept: 🌙   Energy Level: 🔋

- 😁 Very happy
- 🙂 Mostly happy
- 😐 Apathetic
- 😞 Feeling down
- 🙁 Sad
- 😢 Emotional
- 😭 Distressed/crying
- 😷 Sick

Food: _____
_____

What I think prompted this mood: _____
_____
_____

What action can I take for this mood: _____
_____
_____

Physical Activity today: _____
_____

Other Emotions:
Hopeless   Panic attack   Isolated   Lonely   Irritated   Energized   Aggressive   Anger   Other:

• •

EVENING MOOD   Progress towards today's goal: _____

- 😁 Very happy
- 🙂 Mostly happy
- 😐 Apathetic
- 😞 Feeling down
- 🙁 Sad
- 😢 Emotional
- 😭 Distressed/crying
- 😷 Sick

Food: _____
_____

What I think prompted this mood: _____
_____
_____

What action can I take for this mood: _____
_____
_____

Something good that happened today: _____
_____

Other Emotions:
Hopeless   Panic attack   Isolated   Lonely   Irritated   Energized   Aggressive   Anger   Other:

Today I am grateful for: _____

Date: _____ Goal for today: _____

MORNING MOOD

Hours Slept: 🌙

Energy Level: 🔋

😁 Very happy

🙂 Mostly happy

😐 Apathetic

😔 Feeling down

🙁 Sad

😢 Emotional

😭 Distressed/crying

🤢 Sick

Food: _____
_____
_____

What i think prompted this mood: _____
_____
_____

What action can i take for this mood: _____
_____
_____

Physical Activity today: _____
_____

Other Emotions:
Hopeless   Panic attack   Isolated   Lonely   Irritated   Energized   Aggressive   Anger   Other:

• •

EVENING MOOD

Progress towards today's goal: _____

😁 Very happy

🙂 Mostly happy

😐 Apathetic

😔 Feeling down

🙁 Sad

😢 Emotional

😭 Distressed/crying

🤢 Sick

Food: _____
_____
_____

What i think prompted this mood: _____
_____
_____

What action can i take for this mood: _____
_____
_____

Something good that happened today: _____
_____

Other Emotions:
Hopeless   Panic attack   Isolated   Lonely   Irritated   Energized   Aggressive   Anger   Other:

Today I am grateful for: _____

Date: _____   Goal for today: _____

MORNING MOOD

Hours Slept: 🌙   Energy Level: 🔋

😁 Very happy
🙂 Mostly happy
😐 Apathetic
😔 Feeling down
🙁 Sad
😢 Emotional
🏚 Distressed/crying
😷 Sick

Food: _____
_____
_____

What i think prompted this mood: _____
_____
_____

What action can i take for this mood: _____
_____
_____

Physical Activity today: _____
_____

Other Emotions:
Hopeless   Panic attack   Isolated   Lonely   Irritated   Energized   Aggressive   Anger   Other:

• •

EVENING MOOD

Progress towards today's goal: _____

😁 Very happy
🙂 Mostly happy
😐 Apathetic
😔 Feeling down
🙁 Sad
😢 Emotional
🏚 Distressed/crying
😷 Sick

Food: _____
_____
_____

What i think prompted this mood: _____
_____
_____

What action can i take for this mood: _____
_____
_____

Something good that happened today: _____
_____

Other Emotions:
Hopeless   Panic attack   Isolated   Lonely   Irritated   Energized   Aggressive   Anger   Other:

Today I am grateful for: _____

Date: _____ Goal for today: _____

MORNING MOOD

Hours Slept:

Energy Level:

😁 Very happy

🙂 Mostly happy

😐 Apathetic

😔 Feeling down

☹️ Sad

😢 Emotional

😭 Distressed/crying

🤢 Sick

Food: _____
_____
_____

What i think prompted this mood: _____
_____
_____

What action can i take for this mood: _____
_____
_____

Physical Activity today: _____
_____

Other Emotions:
Hopeless   Panic attack   Isolated   Lonely   Irritated   Energized   Aggressive   Anger   Other:

• •

EVENING MOOD

Progress towards today's goal: _____

😁 Very happy

🙂 Mostly happy

😐 Apathetic

😔 Feeling down

☹️ Sad

😢 Emotional

😭 Distressed/crying

🤢 Sick

Food: _____
_____
_____

What i think prompted this mood: _____
_____
_____

What action can i take for this mood: _____
_____
_____

Something good that happened today: _____
_____

Other Emotions:
Hopeless   Panic attack   Isolated   Lonely   Irritated   Energized   Aggressive   Anger   Other:

Today I am grateful for: _____

Date: _____ Goal for today: _____

MORNING MOOD

Hours Slept: 🌙

Energy Level: 🔋

😁 Very happy
🙂 Mostly happy
😐 Apathetic
😞 Feeling down
🙁 Sad
😢 Emotional
😭 Distressed/crying
😷 Sick

Food: _____
_____
_____

What I think prompted this mood: _____
_____
_____

What action can I take for this mood: _____
_____
_____

Physical Activity today: _____
_____

Other Emotions:
Hopeless   Panic attack   Isolated   Lonely   Irritated   Energized   Aggressive   Anger   Other:

• •

EVENING MOOD

Progress towards today's goal: _____

😁 Very happy
🙂 Mostly happy
😐 Apathetic
😞 Feeling down
🙁 Sad
😢 Emotional
😭 Distressed/crying
😷 Sick

Food: _____
_____
_____

What I think prompted this mood: _____
_____
_____

What action can I take for this mood: _____
_____
_____

Something good that happened today: _____

Other Emotions:
Hopeless   Panic attack   Isolated   Lonely   Irritated   Energized   Aggressive   Anger   Other:

Today I am grateful for: _____

Date: _____ Goal for today: _____

MORNING MOOD

Hours Slept:

Energy Level:

- 😁 Very happy
- 🙂 Mostly happy
- 😐 Apathetic
- 😞 Feeling down
- 🙁 Sad
- 😢 Emotional
- 😭 Distressed/crying
- 🤒 Sick

Food: _____
_____
_____

What i think prompted this mood: _____
_____
_____

What action can i take for this mood: _____
_____
_____

Physical Activity today: _____
_____

Other Emotions:
Hopeless Panic attack Isolated Lonely Irritated Energized Aggressive Anger Other:

• •

EVENING MOOD

Progress towards today's goal: _____

- 😁 Very happy
- 🙂 Mostly happy
- 😐 Apathetic
- 😞 Feeling down
- 🙁 Sad
- 😢 Emotional
- 😭 Distressed/crying
- 🤒 Sick

Food: _____
_____
_____

What i think prompted this mood: _____
_____
_____

What action can i take for this mood: _____
_____
_____

Something good that happened today: _____
_____

Other Emotions:
Hopeless Panic attack Isolated Lonely Irritated Energized Aggressive Anger Other:

Today I am grateful for: _____

Date: _____ Goal for today: _____

MORNING MOOD

Hours Slept: 🌙

Energy Level: 🔋

- 😁 Very happy
- 🙂 Mostly happy
- 😐 Apathetic
- 😔 Feeling down
- 🙁 Sad
- 😢 Emotional
- 😭 Distressed/crying
- 🤢 Sick

Food: _____
_____

What I think prompted this mood: _____
_____

What action can I take for this mood: _____
_____

Physical Activity today: _____
_____

Other Emotions:
Hopeless   Panic attack   Isolated   Lonely   Irritated   Energized   Aggressive   Anger   Other:

EVENING MOOD

Progress towards today's goal: _____

- 😁 Very happy
- 🙂 Mostly happy
- 😐 Apathetic
- 😔 Feeling down
- 🙁 Sad
- 😢 Emotional
- 😭 Distressed/crying
- 🤢 Sick

Food: _____
_____

What I think prompted this mood: _____
_____

What action can I take for this mood: _____
_____

Something good that happened today: _____
_____

Other Emotions:
Hopeless   Panic attack   Isolated   Lonely   Irritated   Energized   Aggressive   Anger   Other:

Today I am grateful for: _____

Date: _____ Goal for today: _____

MORNING MOOD

Hours Slept: 🌙   Energy Level: 🔋

😁 Very happy

🙂 Mostly happy

😐 Apathetic

😔 Feeling down

☹️ Sad

😢 Emotional

🏠 Distressed/crying

😣 Sick

Other Emotions:
Hopeless Panic attack Isolated Lonely Irritated Energized Aggressive Anger Other:

Food: _____
_____
_____

What i think prompted this mood: _____
_____
_____

What action can i take for this mood: _____
_____
_____

Physical Activity today: _____
_____

· ·

EVENING MOOD

Progress towards today's goal: _____

😁 Very happy

🙂 Mostly happy

😐 Apathetic

😔 Feeling down

☹️ Sad

😢 Emotional

🏠 Distressed/crying

😣 Sick

Other Emotions:
Hopeless Panic attack Isolated Lonely Irritated Energized Aggressive Anger Other:

Food: _____
_____
_____

What i think prompted this mood: _____
_____
_____

What action can i take for this mood: _____
_____
_____

Something good that happened today: _____
_____

Today I am grateful for: _____

Date: _____ Goal for today: _____

MORNING MOOD

Hours Slept: 🌙

Energy Level: 🔋

😁 Very happy

🙂 Mostly happy

😐 Apathetic

😞 Feeling down

☹️ Sad

😢 Emotional

😭 Distressed/crying

😷 Sick

Food: _____
_____
_____

What I think prompted this mood: _____
_____
_____

What action can I take for this mood: _____
_____
_____

Physical Activity today: _____
_____

Other Emotions:
Hopeless   Panic attack   Isolated   Lonely   Irritated   Energized   Aggressive   Anger   Other:

• •

EVENING MOOD

Progress towards today's goal: _____

😁 Very happy

🙂 Mostly happy

😐 Apathetic

😞 Feeling down

☹️ Sad

😢 Emotional

😭 Distressed/crying

😷 Sick

Food: _____
_____
_____

What I think prompted this mood: _____
_____
_____

What action can I take for this mood: _____
_____
_____

Something good that happened today: _____
_____

Other Emotions:
Hopeless   Panic attack   Isolated   Lonely   Irritated   Energized   Aggressive   Anger   Other:

Today I am grateful for: _____

Date: _____ Goal for today: _____

MORNING MOOD

Hours Slept: 🌙

Energy Level: 🔋

😁 Very happy

🙂 Mostly happy

😐 Apathetic

😔 Feeling down

🙁 Sad

😢 Emotional

😭 Distressed/crying

😷 Sick

Food: _____
_____
_____

What i think prompted this mood: _____
_____
_____

What action can i take for this mood: _____
_____
_____

Physical Activity today: _____
_____

Other Emotions:
Hopeless Panic attack Isolated Lonely Irritated Energized Aggressive Anger Other:

• •

EVENING MOOD

Progress towards today's goal: _____

😁 Very happy

🙂 Mostly happy

😐 Apathetic

😔 Feeling down

🙁 Sad

😢 Emotional

😭 Distressed/crying

😷 Sick

Food: _____
_____
_____

What i think prompted this mood: _____
_____
_____

What action can i take for this mood: _____
_____

Something good that happened today: _____

Other Emotions:
Hopeless Panic attack Isolated Lonely Irritated Energized Aggressive Anger Other:

Today I am grateful for: _____

DATE: _____ GOAL FOR TODAY: _____

MORNING MOOD

HOURS
SLEPT: 🌙

ENERGY
LEVEL: 🔋

😁 VERY HAPPY

🙂 MOSTLY HAPPY

😐 APATHETIC

😔 FEELING DOWN

🙁 SAD

😢 EMOTIONAL

😭 DISTRESSED/CRYING

🤢 SICK

FOOD: _____
_____
_____

WHAT I THINK PROMPTED THIS MOOD: _____
_____
_____

WHAT ACTION CAN I TAKE FOR THIS MOOD: _____
_____
_____

PHYSICAL ACTIVITY TODAY: _____
_____

OTHER EMOTIONS:
HOPELESS   PANIC ATTACK   ISOLATED   LONELY   IRRITATED   ENERGIZED   AGGRESSIVE   ANGER   OTHER:

• •

EVENING MOOD

PROGRESS TOWARDS TODAY'S GOAL: _____

😁 VERY HAPPY

🙂 MOSTLY HAPPY

😐 APATHETIC

😔 FEELING DOWN

🙁 SAD

😢 EMOTIONAL

😭 DISTRESSED/CRYING

🤢 SICK

FOOD: _____
_____
_____

WHAT I THINK PROMPTED THIS MOOD: _____
_____
_____

WHAT ACTION CAN I TAKE FOR THIS MOOD: _____
_____
_____

SOMETHING GOOD THAT HAPPENED TODAY: _____
_____

OTHER EMOTIONS:
HOPELESS   PANIC ATTACK   ISOLATED   LONELY   IRRITATED   ENERGIZED   AGGRESSIVE   ANGER   OTHER:

TODAY I AM GRATEFUL FOR: _____

Date: _____ Goal for today: _____

MORNING MOOD

Hours Slept: 🌙

Energy Level: 🔋

😁 Very happy

🙂 Mostly happy

😐 Apathetic

😔 Feeling down

🙁 Sad

😢 Emotional

🏠 Distressed/crying

😷 sick

Food: _____
_____
_____

What i think prompted this mood: _____
_____
_____

What action can i take for this mood: _____
_____
_____

Physical Activity today: _____
_____

Other Emotions:
Hopeless   Panic attack   Isolated   Lonely   Irritated   Energized   Aggressive   Anger   Other:

• •

EVENING MOOD

Progress towards today's goal: _____

😁 Very happy

🙂 Mostly happy

😐 Apathetic

😔 Feeling down

🙁 Sad

😢 Emotional

🏠 Distressed/crying

😷 sick

Food: _____
_____
_____

What i think prompted this mood: _____
_____
_____

What action can i take for this mood: _____
_____
_____

Something good that happened today: _____
_____

Other Emotions:
Hopeless   Panic attack   Isolated   Lonely   Irritated   Energized   Aggressive   Anger   Other:

Today I am grateful for: _____

Date: _____ Goal for today: _____

MORNING MOOD

Hours Slept: 🌙

Energy Level: 🔋

- 😁 Very happy
- 🙂 Mostly happy
- 😐 Apathetic
- 😔 Feeling down
- 🙁 Sad
- 😢 Emotional
- 😭 Distressed/crying
- 🤢 Sick

Food: _____
_____
_____

What I think prompted this mood: _____
_____
_____

What action can I take for this mood: _____
_____
_____

Physical Activity today: _____
_____

Other Emotions:
Hopeless Panic attack Isolated Lonely Irritated Energized Aggressive Anger Other:

• •

EVENING MOOD

Progress towards today's goal: _____

- 😁 Very happy
- 🙂 Mostly happy
- 😐 Apathetic
- 😔 Feeling down
- 🙁 Sad
- 😢 Emotional
- 😭 Distressed/crying
- 🤢 Sick

Food: _____
_____
_____

What I think prompted this mood: _____
_____
_____

What action can I take for this mood: _____
_____
_____

Something good that happened today: _____
_____

Other Emotions:
Hopeless Panic attack Isolated Lonely Irritated Energized Aggressive Anger Other:

Today I am grateful for: _____

DATE: _____   GOAL FOR TODAY: _____

MORNING MOOD

HOURS SLEPT: 🌙   ENERGY LEVEL: 🔋

- 😁 VERY HAPPY
- 🙂 MOSTLY HAPPY
- 😐 APATHETIC
- 😔 FEELING DOWN
- 🙁 SAD
- 😢 EMOTIONAL
- 😭 DISTRESSED/CRYING
- 🤢 SICK

FOOD: _____
_____
_____

WHAT I THINK PROMPTED THIS MOOD: _____
_____
_____

WHAT ACTION CAN I TAKE FOR THIS MOOD: _____
_____
_____

PHYSICAL ACTIVITY TODAY: _____
_____

OTHER EMOTIONS:
HOPELESS   PANIC ATTACK   ISOLATED   LONELY   IRRITATED   ENERGIZED   AGGRESSIVE   ANGER   OTHER:

• •

EVENING MOOD

PROGRESS TOWARDS TODAY'S GOAL: _____

- 😁 VERY HAPPY
- 🙂 MOSTLY HAPPY
- 😐 APATHETIC
- 😔 FEELING DOWN
- 🙁 SAD
- 😢 EMOTIONAL
- 😭 DISTRESSED/CRYING
- 🤢 SICK

FOOD: _____
_____
_____

WHAT I THINK PROMPTED THIS MOOD: _____
_____
_____

WHAT ACTION CAN I TAKE FOR THIS MOOD: _____
_____
_____

SOMETHING GOOD THAT HAPPENED TODAY: _____
_____

OTHER EMOTIONS:
HOPELESS   PANIC ATTACK   ISOLATED   LONELY   IRRITATED   ENERGIZED   AGGRESSIVE   ANGER   OTHER:

TODAY I AM GRATEFUL FOR: _____

Date: _____ Goal for today: _____

MORNING MOOD

Hours Slept: 🌙   Energy Level: 🔋

- 😁 Very happy
- 🙂 Mostly happy
- 😐 Apathetic
- 😔 Feeling down
- 🙁 Sad
- 😢 Emotional
- 😭 Distressed/crying
- 🤢 Sick

Food: _____
_____

What i think prompted this mood: _____
_____
_____

What action can i take for this mood: _____
_____
_____

Physical Activity today: _____
_____

Other Emotions:
Hopeless   Panic attack   Isolated   Lonely   Irritated   Energized   Aggressive   Anger   Other:

• •

EVENING MOOD

Progress towards today's goal: _____

- 😁 Very happy
- 🙂 Mostly happy
- 😐 Apathetic
- 😔 Feeling down
- 🙁 Sad
- 😢 Emotional
- 😭 Distressed/crying
- 🤢 Sick

Food: _____
_____

What i think prompted this mood: _____
_____
_____

What action can i take for this mood: _____
_____
_____

Something good that happened today: _____
_____

Other Emotions:
Hopeless   Panic attack   Isolated   Lonely   Irritated   Energized   Aggressive   Anger   Other:

Today I am grateful for: _____

Date: _____ Goal for today: _____

MORNING MOOD

Hours Slept:

Energy Level:

😁 Very happy

🙂 Mostly happy

😐 Apathetic

😞 Feeling down

☹️ Sad

😢 Emotional

😭 Distressed/crying

😖 Sick

Food: _____
_____
_____

What i think prompted this mood: _____
_____
_____

What action can i take for this mood: _____
_____
_____

Physical Activity today: _____
_____

Other Emotions:
Hopeless   Panic attack   Isolated   Lonely   Irritated   Energized   Aggressive   Anger   Other:

• •

EVENING MOOD

Progress towards today's goal: _____

😁 Very happy

🙂 Mostly happy

😐 Apathetic

😞 Feeling down

☹️ Sad

😢 Emotional

😭 Distressed/crying

😖 Sick

Food: _____
_____
_____

What i think prompted this mood: _____
_____
_____

What action can i take for this mood: _____
_____

Something good that happened today: _____
_____

Other Emotions:
Hopeless   Panic attack   Isolated   Lonely   Irritated   Energized   Aggressive   Anger   Other:

Today I am grateful for: _____

Date: _____ Goal for today: _____

MORNING MOOD

Hours Slept: 🌙

Energy Level: 🔋

😁 Very happy

🙂 Mostly happy

😐 Apathetic

😣 Feeling down

🙁 Sad

😢 Emotional

😭 Distressed/crying

🤢 Sick

Food: _____
_____

What i think prompted this mood: _____
_____
_____

What action can i take for this mood: _____
_____
_____

Physical Activity today: _____
_____

Other Emotions:
Hopeless   Panic attack   Isolated   Lonely   Irritated   Energized   Aggressive   Anger   Other:

• •

EVENING MOOD

Progress towards today's goal: _____

😁 Very happy

🙂 Mostly happy

😐 Apathetic

😣 Feeling down

🙁 Sad

😢 Emotional

😭 Distressed/crying

🤢 Sick

Food: _____
_____

What i think prompted this mood: _____
_____
_____

What action can i take for this mood: _____
_____
_____

Something good that happened today: _____
_____

Other Emotions:
Hopeless   Panic attack   Isolated   Lonely   Irritated   Energized   Aggressive   Anger   Other:

Today I am grateful for: _____

Date: _____ Goal for today: _____

MORNING MOOD

Hours Slept: Energy Level:

- 😁 Very happy
- 🙂 Mostly happy
- 😐 Apathetic
- 😞 Feeling down
- 🙁 Sad
- 😢 Emotional
- 😭 Distressed/crying
- 😷 Sick

Food: _____
_____
_____

What I think prompted this mood: _____
_____
_____

What action can I take for this mood: _____
_____
_____

Physical Activity today: _____
_____

Other Emotions:
Hopeless Panic attack Isolated Lonely Irritated Energized Aggressive Anger Other:

EVENING MOOD

Progress towards today's goal: _____

- 😁 Very happy
- 🙂 Mostly happy
- 😐 Apathetic
- 😞 Feeling down
- 🙁 Sad
- 😢 Emotional
- 😭 Distressed/crying
- 😷 Sick

Food: _____
_____
_____

What I think prompted this mood: _____
_____
_____

What action can I take for this mood: _____
_____
_____

Something good that happened today: _____
_____

Other Emotions:
Hopeless Panic attack Isolated Lonely Irritated Energized Aggressive Anger Other:

Today I am grateful for: _____

Date: _____   Goal for today: _____

MORNING MOOD

Hours Slept: 🌙   Energy Level: 🔋

- 😁 Very happy
- 🙂 Mostly happy
- 😐 Apathetic
- 😞 Feeling down
- ☹️ Sad
- 😢 Emotional
- 😭 Distressed/crying
- 😷 Sick

Food: _____
_____

What i think prompted this mood: _____
_____
_____

What action can i take for this mood: _____
_____
_____

Physical Activity today: _____

Other Emotions:
Hopeless   Panic attack   Isolated   Lonely   Irritated   Energized   Aggressive   Anger   Other:

● ●

EVENING MOOD

Progress towards today's goal: _____

- 😁 Very happy
- 🙂 Mostly happy
- 😐 Apathetic
- 😞 Feeling down
- ☹️ Sad
- 😢 Emotional
- 😭 Distressed/crying
- 😷 Sick

Food: _____
_____

What i think prompted this mood: _____
_____
_____

What action can i take for this mood: _____
_____
_____

Something good that happened today: _____
_____

Other Emotions:
Hopeless   Panic attack   Isolated   Lonely   Irritated   Energized   Aggressive   Anger   Other:

Today I am grateful for: _____

Date: _____ Goal for today: _____

MORNING MOOD

Hours Slept:

Energy Level:

😁 Very happy

🙂 Mostly happy

😐 Apathetic

😞 Feeling down

☹️ Sad

😢 Emotional

😭 Distressed/crying

😷 Sick

Food: _____
_____
_____

What i think prompted this mood: _____
_____
_____

What action can i take for this mood: _____
_____
_____

Physical Activity today: _____
_____

Other Emotions:
Hopeless Panic attack Isolated Lonely Irritated Energized Aggressive Anger Other:

• •

EVENING MOOD

Progress towards today's goal: _____

😁 Very happy

🙂 Mostly happy

😐 Apathetic

😞 Feeling down

☹️ Sad

😢 Emotional

😭 Distressed/crying

😷 Sick

Food: _____
_____
_____

What i think prompted this mood: _____
_____
_____

What action can i take for this mood: _____
_____
_____

Something good that happened today: _____
_____

Other Emotions:
Hopeless Panic attack Isolated Lonely Irritated Energized Aggressive Anger Other:

Today I am grateful for: _____

Date: _____   Goal for today: _____

MORNING MOOD

Hours Slept: 🌙   Energy Level: 🔋

Mood	
😁	Very happy
🙂	Mostly happy
😐	Apathetic
😔	Feeling down
🙁	Sad
😢	Emotional
😭	Distressed/crying
😷	Sick

Food: _____
_____
_____

What I think prompted this mood: _____
_____
_____

What action can I take for this mood: _____
_____
_____

Physical Activity today: _____
_____

Other Emotions:
Hopeless   Panic attack   Isolated   Lonely   Irritated   Energized   Aggressive   Anger   Other:

• •

EVENING MOOD

Progress towards today's goal: _____

Mood	
😁	Very happy
🙂	Mostly happy
😐	Apathetic
😔	Feeling down
🙁	Sad
😢	Emotional
😭	Distressed/crying
😷	Sick

Food: _____
_____
_____

What I think prompted this mood: _____
_____
_____

What action can I take for this mood: _____
_____
_____

Something good that happened today: _____
_____

Other Emotions:
Hopeless   Panic attack   Isolated   Lonely   Irritated   Energized   Aggressive   Anger   Other:

Today I am grateful for: _____

Date: _____ Goal for today: _____

MORNING MOOD

Hours Slept:

Energy Level:

😁 Very happy

🙂 Mostly happy

😐 Apathetic

😞 Feeling down

🙁 Sad

😢 Emotional

😭 Distressed/crying

😷 Sick

Food: _____
_____
_____

What I think prompted this mood: _____
_____
_____

What action can I take for this mood: _____
_____
_____

Physical Activity today: _____
_____

Other Emotions:
Hopeless   Panic attack   Isolated   Lonely   Irritated   Energized   Aggressive   Anger   Other:

· ◄

EVENING MOOD

Progress towards today's goal: _____

😁 Very happy

🙂 Mostly happy

😐 Apathetic

😞 Feeling down

🙁 Sad

😢 Emotional

😭 Distressed/crying

😷 Sick

Food: _____
_____
_____

What I think prompted this mood: _____
_____
_____

What action can I take for this mood: _____
_____
_____

Something good that happened today: _____
_____

Other Emotions:
Hopeless   Panic attack   Isolated   Lonely   Irritated   Energized   Aggressive   Anger   Other:

Today I am grateful for: _____

Date: _____ Goal for today: _____

MORNING MOOD

Hours Slept: 🌙

Energy Level: 🔋

- 😁 Very happy
- 🙂 Mostly happy
- 😐 Apathetic
- 😞 Feeling down
- 🙁 Sad
- 😢 Emotional
- 😭 Distressed/crying
- 🤢 Sick

Food: _____
_____

What I think prompted this mood: _____
_____
_____

What action can I take for this mood: _____
_____
_____

Physical Activity today: _____
_____

Other Emotions:
Hopeless   Panic attack   Isolated   Lonely   Irritated   Energized   Aggressive   Anger   Other:

• •

EVENING MOOD

Progress towards today's goal: _____

- 😁 Very happy
- 🙂 Mostly happy
- 😐 Apathetic
- 😞 Feeling down
- 🙁 Sad
- 😢 Emotional
- 😭 Distressed/crying
- 🤢 Sick

Food: _____
_____

What I think prompted this mood: _____
_____
_____

What action can I take for this mood: _____
_____
_____

Something good that happened today: _____
_____

Other Emotions:
Hopeless   Panic attack   Isolated   Lonely   Irritated   Energized   Aggressive   Anger   Other:

Today I am grateful for: _____

Date: _____ Goal for today: _____

MORNING MOOD

Hours Slept:

Energy Level:

- 😁 Very happy
- 🙂 Mostly happy
- 😐 Apathetic
- 😔 Feeling down
- ☹️ Sad
- 😢 Emotional
- 😭 Distressed/crying
- 😷 Sick

Food: _____
_____
_____

What i think prompted this mood: _____
_____
_____

What action can i take for this mood: _____
_____
_____

Physical Activity today: _____
_____

Other Emotions:
Hopeless   Panic attack   Isolated   Lonely   Irritated   Energized   Aggressive   Anger   Other:

EVENING MOOD

Progress towards today's goal: _____

- 😁 Very happy
- 🙂 Mostly happy
- 😐 Apathetic
- 😔 Feeling down
- ☹️ Sad
- 😢 Emotional
- 😭 Distressed/crying
- 😷 Sick

Food: _____
_____
_____

What i think prompted this mood: _____
_____
_____

What action can i take for this mood: _____
_____
_____

Something good that happened today: _____
_____

Other Emotions:
Hopeless   Panic attack   Isolated   Lonely   Irritated   Energized   Aggressive   Anger   Other:

Today I am grateful for: _____

Date: _____ Goal for today: _____

MORNING MOOD

Hours Slept: 🌙   Energy Level: 🔋

- 😁 Very happy
- 🙂 Mostly happy
- 😐 Apathetic
- 😞 Feeling down
- ☹️ Sad
- 😢 Emotional
- 😭 Distressed/crying
- 😷 Sick

Food: _____
_____

What i think prompted this mood: _____
_____
_____

What action can i take for this mood: _____
_____
_____

Physical Activity today: _____

Other Emotions:
Hopeless   Panic attack   Isolated   Lonely   Irritated   Energized   Aggressive   Anger   Other:

• •

EVENING MOOD

Progress towards today's goal: _____

- 😁 Very happy
- 🙂 Mostly happy
- 😐 Apathetic
- 😞 Feeling down
- ☹️ Sad
- 😢 Emotional
- 😭 Distressed/crying
- 😷 Sick

Food: _____
_____

What i think prompted this mood: _____
_____
_____

What action can i take for this mood: _____
_____

Something good that happened today: _____
_____

Other Emotions:
Hopeless   Panic attack   Isolated   Lonely   Irritated   Energized   Aggressive   Anger   Other:

Today I am grateful for: _____

DATE: _____ GOAL FOR TODAY: _____

MORNING MOOD

HOURS SLEPT: 🌙   ENERGY LEVEL: 🔋

- 😁 VERY HAPPY
- 🙂 MOSTLY HAPPY
- 😐 APATHETIC
- 😔 FEELING DOWN
- 🙁 SAD
- 😢 EMOTIONAL
- 😭 DISTRESSED/CRYING
- 🤢 SICK

FOOD: _____
_____
_____

WHAT I THINK PROMPTED THIS MOOD: _____
_____
_____

WHAT ACTION CAN I TAKE FOR THIS MOOD: _____
_____
_____

PHYSICAL ACTIVITY TODAY: _____
_____

OTHER EMOTIONS:
HOPELESS   PANIC ATTACK   ISOLATED   LONELY   IRRITATED   ENERGIZED   AGGRESSIVE   ANGER   OTHER:

• •

EVENING MOOD

PROGRESS TOWARDS TODAY'S GOAL: _____

- 😁 VERY HAPPY
- 🙂 MOSTLY HAPPY
- 😐 APATHETIC
- 😔 FEELING DOWN
- 🙁 SAD
- 😢 EMOTIONAL
- 😭 DISTRESSED/CRYING
- 🤢 SICK

FOOD: _____
_____

WHAT I THINK PROMPTED THIS MOOD: _____
_____
_____

WHAT ACTION CAN I TAKE FOR THIS MOOD: _____
_____
_____

SOMETHING GOOD THAT HAPPENED TODAY: _____
_____

OTHER EMOTIONS:
HOPELESS   PANIC ATTACK   ISOLATED   LONELY   IRRITATED   ENERGIZED   AGGRESSIVE   ANGER   OTHER:

TODAY I AM GRATEFUL FOR: _____

Date: _____ Goal for today: _____

MORNING MOOD

Hours Slept: 🌙   Energy Level: 🔋

😄 Very happy

🙂 Mostly happy

😐 Apathetic

😔 Feeling down

🙁 Sad

😢 Emotional

😭 Distressed/crying

😷 Sick

Food: _____

_____

_____

What i think prompted this mood: _____

_____

_____

What action can i take for this mood: _____

_____

_____

Physical Activity today: _____

_____

Other Emotions:

Hopeless   Panic attack   Isolated   Lonely   Irritated   Energized   Aggressive   Anger   Other:

• •

EVENING MOOD

Progress towards today's goal: _____

😄 Very happy

🙂 Mostly happy

😐 Apathetic

😔 Feeling down

🙁 Sad

😢 Emotional

😭 Distressed/crying

😷 Sick

Food: _____

_____

_____

What i think prompted this mood: _____

_____

_____

What action can i take for this mood: _____

_____

_____

Something good that happened today: _____

_____

Other Emotions:

Hopeless   Panic attack   Isolated   Lonely   Irritated   Energized   Aggressive   Anger   Other:

Today i am grateful for: _____

Date: _____ Goal for today: _____

MORNING MOOD

Hours Slept:

Energy Level:

- 😁 Very happy
- 🙂 Mostly happy
- 😐 Apathetic
- 😣 Feeling down
- 😟 Sad
- 😢 Emotional
- 😭 Distressed/crying
- 😷 Sick

Food: _____
_____
_____

What I think prompted this mood: _____
_____
_____

What action can I take for this mood: _____
_____
_____

Physical Activity today: _____
_____

Other Emotions:

Hopeless   Panic attack   Isolated   Lonely   Irritated   Energized   Aggressive   Anger   Other:

• •

EVENING MOOD

Progress towards today's goal: _____

- 😁 Very happy
- 🙂 Mostly happy
- 😐 Apathetic
- 😣 Feeling down
- 😟 Sad
- 😢 Emotional
- 😭 Distressed/crying
- 😷 Sick

Food: _____
_____

What I think prompted this mood: _____
_____
_____

What action can I take for this mood: _____
_____
_____

Something good that happened today: _____
_____

Other Emotions:

Hopeless   Panic attack   Isolated   Lonely   Irritated   Energized   Aggressive   Anger   Other:

Today I am grateful for: _____

Date: _____ Goal for today: _____

MORNING MOOD

Hours Slept: 🌙

Energy Level: 🔋

😁 Very happy

🙂 Mostly happy

😐 Apathetic

😞 Feeling down

🙁 Sad

😢 Emotional

🏠 Distressed/crying

😷 Sick

Food: _____
_____
_____

What i think prompted this mood: _____
_____
_____

What action can i take for this mood: _____
_____
_____

Physical Activity today: _____

Other Emotions:
_____

Hopeless   Panic attack   Isolated   Lonely   Irritated   Energized   Aggressive   Anger   Other:

• •

EVENING MOOD

Progress towards today's goal: _____

😁 Very happy

🙂 Mostly happy

😐 Apathetic

😞 Feeling down

🙁 Sad

😢 Emotional

🏠 Distressed/crying

😷 Sick

Food: _____
_____

What i think prompted this mood: _____
_____
_____

What action can i take for this mood: _____
_____

Something good that happened today: _____
_____

Other Emotions:

Hopeless   Panic attack   Isolated   Lonely   Irritated   Energized   Aggressive   Anger   Other:

Today I am grateful for: _____

Date: _____ Goal for today: _____

MORNING MOOD

Hours Slept:

Energy Level:

😃 Very happy

🙂 Mostly happy

😐 Apathetic

😔 Feeling down

🙁 Sad

😢 Emotional

😭 Distressed/crying

😷 Sick

Food: _____
_____
_____

What i think prompted this mood: _____
_____
_____

What action can i take for this mood: _____
_____
_____

Physical Activity today: _____
_____

Other Emotions:
Hopeless Panic attack Isolated Lonely Irritated Energized Aggressive Anger Other:

• •

EVENING MOOD

Progress towards today's goal: _____

😃 Very happy

🙂 Mostly happy

😐 Apathetic

😔 Feeling down

🙁 Sad

😢 Emotional

😭 Distressed/crying

😷 Sick

Food: _____
_____
_____

What i think prompted this mood: _____
_____
_____

What action can i take for this mood: _____
_____
_____

Something good that happened today: _____
_____

Other Emotions:
Hopeless Panic attack Isolated Lonely Irritated Energized Aggressive Anger Other:

Today I am grateful for: _____

Date: _____ Goal for today: _____

MORNING MOOD

Hours Slept:

Energy Level:

- 😁 Very happy
- 🙂 Mostly happy
- 😐 Apathetic
- 😔 Feeling down
- ☹️ Sad
- 😢 Emotional
- 😭 Distressed/crying
- 😷 Sick

Food: _____
_____
_____

What i think prompted this mood: _____
_____
_____

What action can i take for this mood: _____
_____
_____

Physical Activity today: _____
_____

Other Emotions:
Hopeless   Panic attack   Isolated   Lonely   Irritated   Energized   Aggressive   Anger   Other:

• •

EVENING MOOD

Progress towards today's goal: _____

- 😁 Very happy
- 🙂 Mostly happy
- 😐 Apathetic
- 😔 Feeling down
- ☹️ Sad
- 😢 Emotional
- 😭 Distressed/crying
- 😷 Sick

Food: _____
_____
_____

What i think prompted this mood: _____
_____
_____

What action can i take for this mood: _____
_____
_____

Something good that happened today: _____
_____

Other Emotions:
Hopeless   Panic attack   Isolated   Lonely   Irritated   Energized   Aggressive   Anger   Other:

Today I am grateful for: _____

Date: _____ Goal for today: _____

MORNING MOOD

Hours Slept: 🌙

Energy Level: 🔋

😁 Very happy
🙂 Mostly happy
😐 Apathetic
😔 Feeling down
☹️ Sad
😢 Emotional
😭 Distressed/crying
😩 Sick

Food: _____
_____
_____

What i think prompted this mood: _____
_____
_____

What action can i take for this mood: _____
_____
_____

Physical Activity today: _____
_____

Other Emotions:
Hopeless   Panic attack   Isolated   Lonely   Irritated   Energized   Aggressive   Anger   Other:

• •

EVENING MOOD

Progress towards today's goal: _____

😁 Very happy
🙂 Mostly happy
😐 Apathetic
😔 Feeling down
☹️ Sad
😢 Emotional
😭 Distressed/crying
😩 Sick

Food: _____
_____
_____

What i think prompted this mood: _____
_____
_____

What action can i take for this mood: _____
_____
_____

Something good that happened today: _____
_____

Other Emotions:
Hopeless   Panic attack   Isolated   Lonely   Irritated   Energized   Aggressive   Anger   Other:

Today I am grateful for: _____

Date: _____ Goal for today: _____

MORNING MOOD

Hours Slept: 🌙

Energy Level: 🔋

😁 Very happy

🙂 Mostly happy

😐 Apathetic

😔 Feeling down

☹️ Sad

😢 Emotional

😭 Distressed/crying

😷 Sick

Food: _____
_____
_____

What i think prompted this mood: _____
_____
_____

What action can i take for this mood: _____
_____
_____

Physical Activity today: _____
_____

Other Emotions:
Hopeless   Panic attack   Isolated   Lonely   Irritated   Energized   Aggressive   Anger   Other:

• •

EVENING MOOD

Progress towards today's goal: _____

😁 Very happy

🙂 Mostly happy

😐 Apathetic

😔 Feeling down

☹️ Sad

😢 Emotional

😭 Distressed/crying

😷 Sick

Food: _____
_____
_____

What i think prompted this mood: _____
_____
_____

What action can i take for this mood: _____
_____
_____

Something good that happened today: _____
_____

Other Emotions:
Hopeless   Panic attack   Isolated   Lonely   Irritated   Energized   Aggressive   Anger   Other:

Today I am grateful for: _____

Date: _____ Goal for today: _____

MORNING MOOD

Hours Slept:

Energy Level:

😁 Very happy

🙂 Mostly happy

😐 Apathetic

😔 Feeling down

🙁 Sad

😢 Emotional

😭 Distressed/crying

🤒 Sick

Food: _____
_____

What i think prompted this mood: _____
_____
_____

What action can i take for this mood: _____
_____
_____

Physical Activity today: _____
_____

Other Emotions:
Hopeless   Panic attack   Isolated   Lonely   Irritated   Energized   Aggressive   Anger   Other:

EVENING MOOD

Progress towards today's goal: _____

😁 Very happy

🙂 Mostly happy

😐 Apathetic

😔 Feeling down

🙁 Sad

😢 Emotional

😭 Distressed/crying

🤒 Sick

Food: _____
_____

What i think prompted this mood: _____
_____

What action can i take for this mood: _____
_____

Something good that happened today: _____
_____

Other Emotions:
Hopeless   Panic attack   Isolated   Lonely   Irritated   Energized   Aggressive   Anger   Other:

Today I am grateful for: _____

Date: _____ Goal for today: _____

MORNING MOOD

Hours Slept: 🌙

Energy Level: 🔋

😁 Very happy

🙂 Mostly happy

😐 Apathetic

😔 Feeling down

🙁 Sad

😢 Emotional

😭 Distressed/crying

😷 Sick

Food: _____

_____

_____

What i think prompted this mood: _____

_____

_____

What action can i take for this mood: _____

_____

_____

Physical Activity today: _____

_____

Other Emotions:

Hopeless   Panic attack   Isolated   Lonely   Irritated   Energized   Aggressive   Anger   Other:

• •

EVENING MOOD

Progress towards today's goal: _____

😁 Very happy

🙂 Mostly happy

😐 Apathetic

😔 Feeling down

🙁 Sad

😢 Emotional

😭 Distressed/crying

😷 Sick

Food: _____

_____

_____

What i think prompted this mood: _____

_____

_____

What action can i take for this mood: _____

_____

_____

Something good that happened today: _____

_____

Other Emotions:

Hopeless   Panic attack   Isolated   Lonely   Irritated   Energized   Aggressive   Anger   Other:

Today i am grateful for: _____

Date: _____ Goal for today: _____

MORNING MOOD

Hours Slept: 🌙 Energy Level: 🔋

😁 Very happy

🙂 Mostly happy

😐 Apathetic

😔 Feeling down

🙁 Sad

😢 Emotional

😭 Distressed/crying

😷 Sick

Food: _____
_____
_____

What i think prompted this mood: _____
_____
_____

What action can i take for this mood: _____
_____
_____

Physical Activity today: _____
_____

Other Emotions:
Hopeless   Panic attack   Isolated   Lonely   Irritated   Energized   Aggressive   Anger   Other:

· ·

EVENING MOOD

Progress towards today's goal: _____

😁 Very happy

🙂 Mostly happy

😐 Apathetic

😔 Feeling down

🙁 Sad

😢 Emotional

😭 Distressed/crying

😷 Sick

Food: _____
_____

What i think prompted this mood: _____
_____
_____

What action can i take for this mood: _____
_____

Something good that happened today: _____
_____

Other Emotions:
Hopeless   Panic attack   Isolated   Lonely   Irritated   Energized   Aggressive   Anger   Other:

Today I am grateful for: _____

Date: _____ Goal for today: _____

MORNING MOOD

Hours Slept: 🌙   Energy Level: 🔋

😁 Very happy
🙂 Mostly happy
😐 Apathetic
😔 Feeling down
☹️ Sad
😢 Emotional
🏚️ Distressed/crying
😷 Sick

Food: _____

What I think prompted this mood: _____
_____
_____

What action can I take for this mood: _____
_____
_____

Physical Activity today: _____
_____

Other Emotions:
Hopeless   Panic attack   Isolated   Lonely   Irritated   Energized   Aggressive   Anger   Other:

• •

EVENING MOOD

Progress towards today's goal: _____

😁 Very happy
🙂 Mostly happy
😐 Apathetic
😔 Feeling down
☹️ Sad
😢 Emotional
🏚️ Distressed/crying
😷 Sick

Food: _____
_____

What I think prompted this mood: _____
_____
_____

What action can I take for this mood: _____
_____

Something good that happened today: _____
_____

Other Emotions:
Hopeless   Panic attack   Isolated   Lonely   Irritated   Energized   Aggressive   Anger   Other:

Today I am grateful for: _____

Date: _____ Goal for today: _____

MORNING MOOD

Hours Slept:

Energy Level:

- 😁 Very happy
- 🙂 Mostly happy
- 😐 Apathetic
- 😔 Feeling down
- 🙁 Sad
- 😢 Emotional
- 😭 Distressed/crying
- 😷 Sick

Food: _____
_____
_____

What i think prompted this mood: _____
_____
_____

What action can i take for this mood: _____
_____
_____

Physical Activity today: _____
_____

Other Emotions:
Hopeless   Panic attack   Isolated   Lonely   Irritated   Energized   Aggressive   Anger   Other:

• •

EVENING MOOD

Progress towards today's goal: _____

- 😁 Very happy
- 🙂 Mostly happy
- 😐 Apathetic
- 😔 Feeling down
- 🙁 Sad
- 😢 Emotional
- 😭 Distressed/crying
- 😷 Sick

Food: _____
_____
_____

What i think prompted this mood: _____
_____
_____

What action can i take for this mood: _____
_____
_____

Something good that happened today: _____

Other Emotions:
Hopeless   Panic attack   Isolated   Lonely   Irritated   Energized   Aggressive   Anger   Other:

Today I am grateful for: _____

Date: _____ Goal for today: _____

MORNING MOOD

Hours Slept: 🌙　　Energy Level: 🔋

😁 Very happy

🙂 Mostly happy

😐 Apathetic

😔 Feeling down

🙁 Sad

😢 Emotional

🏠 Distressed/crying

😷 Sick

Food: _____

_____

What i think prompted this mood: _____

_____

_____

What action can i take for this mood: _____

_____

_____

Physical Activity today: _____

_____

Other Emotions:

Hopeless　Panic attack　Isolated　Lonely　Irritated　Energized　Aggressive　Anger　Other:

● ●

EVENING MOOD

Progress towards today's goal: _____

😁 Very happy

🙂 Mostly happy

😐 Apathetic

😔 Feeling down

🙁 Sad

😢 Emotional

🏠 Distressed/crying

😷 Sick

Food: _____

_____

_____

What i think prompted this mood: _____

_____

_____

What action can i take for this mood: _____

_____

_____

Something good that happened today: _____

_____

Other Emotions:

Hopeless　Panic attack　Isolated　Lonely　Irritated　Energized　Aggressive　Anger　Other:

Today I am grateful for: _____

Date: _____ Goal for today: _____

MORNING MOOD

Hours Slept:

Energy Level:

- 😄 Very happy
- 🙂 Mostly happy
- 😐 Apathetic
- 😣 Feeling down
- 🙁 Sad
- 😢 Emotional
- 😭 Distressed/crying
- 😷 Sick

Food: _____
_____

What i think prompted this mood: _____
_____
_____

What action can i take for this mood: _____
_____
_____

Physical Activity today: _____
_____

Other Emotions:
Hopeless   Panic attack   Isolated   Lonely   Irritated   Energized   Aggressive   Anger   Other:

• •

EVENING MOOD

Progress towards today's goal: _____

- 😄 Very happy
- 🙂 Mostly happy
- 😐 Apathetic
- 😣 Feeling down
- 🙁 Sad
- 😢 Emotional
- 😭 Distressed/crying
- 😷 Sick

Food: _____
_____

What i think prompted this mood: _____
_____
_____

What action can i take for this mood: _____
_____
_____

Something good that happened today: _____
_____

Other Emotions:
Hopeless   Panic attack   Isolated   Lonely   Irritated   Energized   Aggressive   Anger   Other:

Today I am grateful for: _____

Date: _____ Goal for today: _____

MORNING MOOD

Hours Slept: 🌓 Energy Level: 🔋

😁 Very happy
🙂 Mostly happy
😐 Apathetic
😞 Feeling down
🙁 Sad
😢 Emotional
😭 Distressed/crying
🤢 Sick

Food: _____
_____
_____

What i think prompted this mood: _____
_____
_____

What action can i take for this mood: _____
_____

Physical Activity today: _____
_____

Other Emotions:
Hopeless   Panic attack   Isolated   Lonely   Irritated   Energized   Aggressive   Anger   Other:

• •

EVENING MOOD

Progress towards today's goal: _____

😁 Very happy
🙂 Mostly happy
😐 Apathetic
😞 Feeling down
🙁 Sad
😢 Emotional
😭 Distressed/crying
🤢 Sick

Food: _____
_____

What i think prompted this mood: _____
_____
_____

What action can i take for this mood: _____
_____

Something good that happened today: _____
_____

Other Emotions:
Hopeless   Panic attack   Isolated   Lonely   Irritated   Energized   Aggressive   Anger   Other:

Today I am grateful for: _____

Date: _____ Goal for today: _____

MORNING MOOD

Hours Slept: 🌙   Energy Level: 🔋

- 😁 Very happy
- 🙂 Mostly happy
- 😐 Apathetic
- 😞 Feeling down
- 🙁 Sad
- 😢 Emotional
- 😭 Distressed/crying
- 😷 Sick

Food: _____
_____
_____

What i think prompted this mood: _____
_____
_____

What action can i take for this mood: _____
_____
_____

Physical Activity today: _____
_____

Other Emotions:
Hopeless Panic attack Isolated Lonely Irritated Energized Aggressive Anger Other:

• •

EVENING MOOD

Progress towards today's goal: _____

- 😁 Very happy
- 🙂 Mostly happy
- 😐 Apathetic
- 😞 Feeling down
- 🙁 Sad
- 😢 Emotional
- 😭 Distressed/crying
- 😷 Sick

Food: _____
_____
_____

What i think prompted this mood: _____
_____
_____

What action can i take for this mood: _____
_____
_____

Something good that happened today: _____
_____

Other Emotions:
Hopeless Panic attack Isolated Lonely Irritated Energized Aggressive Anger Other:

Today I am grateful for: _____

Date: _____   Goal for today: _____

MORNING MOOD

Hours Slept: 🌙

Energy Level: 🔋

- 😁 Very happy
- 🙂 Mostly happy
- 😐 Apathetic
- 😔 Feeling down
- 🙁 Sad
- 😢 Emotional
- 😭 Distressed/crying
- 😣 Sick

Food: _____
_____

What I think prompted this mood: _____
_____
_____

What action can I take for this mood: _____
_____
_____

Physical Activity today: _____
_____

Other Emotions:
Hopeless   Panic attack   Isolated   Lonely   Irritated   Energized   Aggressive   Anger   Other:

•••

EVENING MOOD

Progress towards today's goal: _____

- 😁 Very happy
- 🙂 Mostly happy
- 😐 Apathetic
- 😔 Feeling down
- 🙁 Sad
- 😢 Emotional
- 😭 Distressed/crying
- 😣 Sick

Food: _____
_____
_____

What I think prompted this mood: _____
_____
_____

What action can I take for this mood: _____
_____

Something good that happened today: _____
_____

Other Emotions:
Hopeless   Panic attack   Isolated   Lonely   Irritated   Energized   Aggressive   Anger   Other:

Today I am grateful for: _____

Date: _____ Goal for today: _____

MORNING MOOD

Hours Slept: 🌙

Energy Level: 🔋

😁 Very happy
🙂 Mostly happy
😐 Apathetic
😔 Feeling down
🙁 Sad
😢 Emotional
🏠 Distressed/crying
😖 Sick

Other Emotions:
Hopeless   Panic attack   Isolated   Lonely   Irritated   Energized   Aggressive   Anger   Other:

Food: _____
_____
_____

What I think prompted this mood: _____
_____
_____

What action can I take for this mood: _____
_____
_____

Physical Activity today: _____
_____

EVENING MOOD

Progress towards today's goal: _____

😁 Very happy
🙂 Mostly happy
😐 Apathetic
😔 Feeling down
🙁 Sad
😢 Emotional
🏠 Distressed/crying
😖 Sick

Other Emotions:
Hopeless   Panic attack   Isolated   Lonely   Irritated   Energized   Aggressive   Anger   Other:

Food: _____
_____
_____

What I think prompted this mood: _____
_____
_____

What action can I take for this mood: _____
_____
_____

Something good that happened today: _____
_____

Today I am grateful for: _____

Date: _____ Goal for today: _____

MORNING MOOD

Hours Slept:

Energy Level:

- 😁 Very happy
- 🙂 Mostly happy
- 😐 Apathetic
- 😔 Feeling down
- 🙁 Sad
- 😢 Emotional
- 😭 Distressed/crying
- 😷 Sick

Food: _____
_____
_____

What I think prompted this mood: _____
_____
_____

What action can I take for this mood: _____
_____
_____

Physical Activity today: _____
_____

Other Emotions:
Hopeless   Panic attack   Isolated   Lonely   Irritated   Energized   Aggressive   Anger   Other:

• •

EVENING MOOD

Progress towards today's goal: _____

- 😁 Very happy
- 🙂 Mostly happy
- 😐 Apathetic
- 😔 Feeling down
- 🙁 Sad
- 😢 Emotional
- 😭 Distressed/crying
- 😷 Sick

Food: _____
_____
_____

What I think prompted this mood: _____
_____
_____

What action can I take for this mood: _____
_____
_____

Something good that happened today: _____
_____

Other Emotions:
Hopeless   Panic attack   Isolated   Lonely   Irritated   Energized   Aggressive   Anger   Other:

Today I am grateful for: _____

Date: _____ Goal for today: _____

MORNING MOOD

Hours Slept:

Energy Level:

😁 Very happy

🙂 Mostly happy

😐 Apathetic

😞 Feeling down

🙁 Sad

😢 Emotional

😭 Distressed/crying

😷 Sick

Food: _____
_____

What i think prompted this mood: _____
_____
_____

What action can i take for this mood: _____
_____
_____

Physical Activity today: _____

Other Emotions:
Hopeless   Panic attack   Isolated   Lonely   Irritated   Energized   Aggressive   Anger   Other:

• •

EVENING MOOD

Progress towards today's goal: _____

😁 Very happy

🙂 Mostly happy

😐 Apathetic

😞 Feeling down

🙁 Sad

😢 Emotional

😭 Distressed/crying

😷 Sick

Food: _____
_____
_____

What i think prompted this mood: _____
_____
_____

What action can i take for this mood: _____
_____

Something good that happened today: _____
_____

Other Emotions:
Hopeless   Panic attack   Isolated   Lonely   Irritated   Energized   Aggressive   Anger   Other:

Today I am grateful for: _____

Date: _____ Goal for today: _____

MORNING MOOD

Hours Slept: 🌙

Energy Level: 🔋

😁 Very happy
🙂 Mostly happy
😐 Apathetic
😔 Feeling down
☹️ Sad
😢 Emotional
🏠 Distressed/crying
😷 sick

Food: _____
_____
_____

What i think prompted this mood: _____
_____
_____

What action can i take for this mood: _____
_____
_____

Physical Activity today: _____

Other Emotions:
_____
Hopeless   Panic attack   Isolated   Lonely   Irritated   Energized   Aggressive   Anger   Other:

• •

EVENING MOOD

Progress towards today's goal: _____

😁 Very happy
🙂 Mostly happy
😐 Apathetic
😔 Feeling down
☹️ Sad
😢 Emotional
🏠 Distressed/crying
😷 sick

Food: _____
_____

What i think prompted this mood: _____
_____
_____

What action can i take for this mood: _____
_____

Something good that happened today: _____
_____

Other Emotions:
Hopeless   Panic attack   Isolated   Lonely   Irritated   Energized   Aggressive   Anger   Other:

Today I am grateful for: _____

Date: _____ Goal for today: _____

MORNING MOOD

Hours Slept:

Energy Level:

😄 Very happy

🙂 Mostly happy

😐 Apathetic

😞 Feeling down

☹️ Sad

😢 Emotional

😭 Distressed/crying

😷 Sick

Food: _____
_____
_____

What i think prompted this mood: _____
_____
_____

What action can i take for this mood: _____
_____
_____

Physical Activity today: _____
_____

Other Emotions:
Hopeless   Panic attack   Isolated   Lonely   Irritated   Energized   Aggressive   Anger   Other:

EVENING MOOD

Progress towards today's goal: _____

😄 Very happy

🙂 Mostly happy

😐 Apathetic

😞 Feeling down

☹️ Sad

😢 Emotional

😭 Distressed/crying

😷 Sick

Food: _____
_____
_____

What i think prompted this mood: _____
_____
_____

What action can i take for this mood: _____
_____
_____

Something good that happened today: _____
_____

Other Emotions:
Hopeless   Panic attack   Isolated   Lonely   Irritated   Energized   Aggressive   Anger   Other:

Today I am grateful for: _____

Date: _____ Goal for today: _____

MORNING MOOD

Hours Slept:

Energy Level:

😁 Very happy

🙂 Mostly happy

😐 Apathetic

😟 Feeling down

🙁 Sad

😢 Emotional

😭 Distressed/crying

😷 Sick

Food: _____

_____

What I think prompted this mood: _____

_____

_____

What action can I take for this mood: _____

_____

_____

Physical Activity today: _____

Other Emotions:

Hopeless   Panic attack   Isolated   Lonely   Irritated   Energized   Aggressive   Anger   Other:

• •

EVENING MOOD

Progress towards today's goal: _____

😁 Very happy

🙂 Mostly happy

😐 Apathetic

😟 Feeling down

🙁 Sad

😢 Emotional

😭 Distressed/crying

😷 Sick

Food: _____

_____

What I think prompted this mood: _____

_____

_____

What action can I take for this mood: _____

_____

_____

Something good that happened today: _____

Other Emotions:

Hopeless   Panic attack   Isolated   Lonely   Irritated   Energized   Aggressive   Anger   Other:

Today I am grateful for: _____

Date: _____ Goal for today: _____

MORNING MOOD

Hours Slept:

Energy Level:

- 😄 Very happy
- 🙂 Mostly happy
- 😐 Apathetic
- 😔 Feeling down
- 🙁 Sad
- 😢 Emotional
- 😭 Distressed/crying
- 😷 Sick

Food: _____
_____
_____

What i think prompted this mood: _____
_____
_____

What action can i take for this mood: _____
_____
_____

Physical Activity today: _____
_____

Other Emotions:
Hopeless   Panic attack   Isolated   Lonely   Irritated   Energized   Aggressive   Anger   Other:

• •

EVENING MOOD

Progress towards today's goal: _____

- 😄 Very happy
- 🙂 Mostly happy
- 😐 Apathetic
- 😔 Feeling down
- 🙁 Sad
- 😢 Emotional
- 😭 Distressed/crying
- 😷 Sick

Food: _____
_____
_____

What i think prompted this mood: _____
_____
_____

What action can i take for this mood: _____
_____
_____

Something good that happened today: _____
_____

Other Emotions:
Hopeless   Panic attack   Isolated   Lonely   Irritated   Energized   Aggressive   Anger   Other:

Today I am grateful for: _____

Date: _____ Goal for today: _____

MORNING MOOD

Hours Slept: 🌙

Energy Level: 🔋

- 😁 Very happy
- 🙂 Mostly happy
- 😐 Apathetic
- 😔 Feeling down
- ☹️ Sad
- 😢 Emotional
- 😭 Distressed/crying
- 🤢 Sick

Food: _____
_____
_____

What i think prompted this mood: _____
_____
_____

What action can i take for this mood: _____
_____
_____

Physical Activity today: _____
_____

Other Emotions:
Hopeless   Panic attack   Isolated   Lonely   Irritated   Energized   Aggressive   Anger   Other:

• •

EVENING MOOD

Progress towards today's goal: _____

- 😁 Very happy
- 🙂 Mostly happy
- 😐 Apathetic
- 😔 Feeling down
- ☹️ Sad
- 😢 Emotional
- 😭 Distressed/crying
- 🤢 Sick

Food: _____
_____
_____

What i think prompted this mood: _____
_____
_____

What action can i take for this mood: _____
_____
_____

Something good that happened today: _____
_____

Other Emotions:
Hopeless   Panic attack   Isolated   Lonely   Irritated   Energized   Aggressive   Anger   Other:

Today I am grateful for: _____

Date: _____ Goal for today: _____

MORNING MOOD

Hours Slept: 🌙   Energy Level: 🔋

😁 Very happy

🙂 Mostly happy

😐 Apathetic

😔 Feeling down

☹️ Sad

😢 Emotional

🏠 Distressed/crying

😷 Sick

Food: _____
_____
_____

What I think prompted this mood: _____
_____
_____

What action can I take for this mood: _____
_____
_____

Physical Activity today: _____
_____

Other Emotions:
Hopeless   Panic attack   Isolated   Lonely   Irritated   Energized   Aggressive   Anger   Other:

• •

EVENING MOOD   Progress towards today's goal: _____

😁 Very happy

🙂 Mostly happy

😐 Apathetic

😔 Feeling down

☹️ Sad

😢 Emotional

🏠 Distressed/crying

😷 Sick

Food: _____
_____
_____

What I think prompted this mood: _____
_____
_____

What action can I take for this mood: _____
_____
_____

Something good that happened today: _____
_____

Other Emotions:
Hopeless   Panic attack   Isolated   Lonely   Irritated   Energized   Aggressive   Anger   Other:

Today I am grateful for: _____

Date: _____   Goal for today: _____

MORNING MOOD

Hours Slept: 🌙   Energy Level: 🔋

😁 Very happy
🙂 Mostly happy
😐 Apathetic
😔 Feeling down
☹️ Sad
😢 Emotional
😭 Distressed/crying
😷 Sick

Food: _____
_____
_____

What I think prompted this mood: _____
_____
_____

What action can I take for this mood: _____
_____
_____

Physical Activity today: _____
_____

Other Emotions:
Hopeless   Panic attack   Isolated   Lonely   Irritated   Energized   Aggressive   Anger   Other:

· ·

EVENING MOOD

Progress towards today's goal: _____

😁 Very happy
🙂 Mostly happy
😐 Apathetic
😔 Feeling down
☹️ Sad
😢 Emotional
😭 Distressed/crying
😷 Sick

Food: _____
_____
_____

What I think prompted this mood: _____
_____
_____

What action can I take for this mood: _____
_____

Something good that happened today: _____
_____

Other Emotions:
Hopeless   Panic attack   Isolated   Lonely   Irritated   Energized   Aggressive   Anger   Other:

Today I am grateful for: _____

DATE: _____ GOAL FOR TODAY: _____

MORNING MOOD

HOURS
SLEPT:

ENERGY
LEVEL:

😄 VERY HAPPY

FOOD: _____
_____
_____

🙂 MOSTLY HAPPY

😐 APATHETIC

WHAT I THINK PROMPTED THIS MOOD: _____
_____
_____

😔 FEELING DOWN

🙁 SAD

😢 EMOTIONAL

WHAT ACTION CAN I TAKE FOR THIS MOOD: _____
_____
_____

😭 DISTRESSED/CRYING

😷 SICK

PHYSICAL ACTIVITY TODAY: _____
_____

OTHER EMOTIONS:
HOPELESS   PANIC ATTACK   ISOLATED   LONELY   IRRITATED   ENERGIZED   AGGRESSIVE   ANGER   OTHER:

• •

EVENING MOOD

PROGRESS TOWARDS TODAY'S GOAL: _____

😄 VERY HAPPY

FOOD: _____
_____
_____

🙂 MOSTLY HAPPY

😐 APATHETIC

WHAT I THINK PROMPTED THIS MOOD: _____
_____
_____

😔 FEELING DOWN

🙁 SAD

😢 EMOTIONAL

WHAT ACTION CAN I TAKE FOR THIS MOOD: _____
_____
_____

😭 DISTRESSED/CRYING

😷 SICK

SOMETHING GOOD THAT HAPPENED TODAY: _____
_____

OTHER EMOTIONS:
HOPELESS   PANIC ATTACK   ISOLATED   LONELY   IRRITATED   ENERGIZED   AGGRESSIVE   ANGER   OTHER:

TODAY I AM GRATEFUL FOR: _____

Date: _____ Goal for today: _____

MORNING MOOD

Hours Slept: 🌙

Energy Level: 🔋

😁 Very happy

🙂 Mostly happy

😐 Apathetic

😞 Feeling down

☹️ Sad

😢 Emotional

🏠 Distressed/crying

😷 Sick

Food: _____
_____

What I think prompted this mood: _____
_____
_____

What action can I take for this mood: _____
_____
_____

Physical Activity today: _____
_____

Other Emotions:
Hopeless   Panic attack   Isolated   Lonely   Irritated   Energized   Aggressive   Anger   Other:

• •

EVENING MOOD

Progress towards today's goal: _____

😁 Very happy

🙂 Mostly happy

😐 Apathetic

😞 Feeling down

☹️ Sad

😢 Emotional

🏠 Distressed/crying

😷 Sick

Food: _____
_____

What I think prompted this mood: _____
_____
_____

What action can I take for this mood: _____
_____
_____

Something good that happened today: _____
_____

Other Emotions:
Hopeless   Panic attack   Isolated   Lonely   Irritated   Energized   Aggressive   Anger   Other:

Today I am grateful for: _____

Date: _____ Goal for today: _____

MORNING MOOD

Hours Slept: 🌙

Energy Level: 🔋

😁 Very happy

🙂 Mostly happy

😐 Apathetic

😣 Feeling down

🙁 Sad

😢 Emotional

😭 Distressed/crying

😷 Sick

Food: _____
_____
_____

What I think prompted this mood: _____
_____
_____

What action can I take for this mood: _____
_____
_____

Physical Activity today: _____
_____

Other Emotions:
Hopeless   Panic attack   Isolated   Lonely   Irritated   Energized   Aggressive   Anger   Other:

· ·

EVENING MOOD

Progress towards today's goal: _____

😁 Very happy

🙂 Mostly happy

😐 Apathetic

😣 Feeling down

🙁 Sad

😢 Emotional

😭 Distressed/crying

😷 Sick

Food: _____
_____
_____

What I think prompted this mood: _____
_____
_____

What action can I take for this mood: _____
_____
_____

Something good that happened today: _____
_____

Other Emotions:
Hopeless   Panic attack   Isolated   Lonely   Irritated   Energized   Aggressive   Anger   Other:

Today I am grateful for: _____

Date: _____ Goal for today: _____

MORNING MOOD

Hours Slept:

Energy Level:

😁 Very happy

🙂 Mostly happy

😐 Apathetic

😔 Feeling down

☹️ Sad

😢 Emotional

😭 Distressed/crying

🤢 Sick

Food: _____
_____
_____

What i think prompted this mood: _____
_____
_____

What action can i take for this mood: _____
_____
_____

Physical Activity today: _____
_____

Other Emotions:
Hopeless   Panic attack   Isolated   Lonely   Irritated   Energized   Aggressive   Anger   Other:

· ·

EVENING MOOD

Progress towards today's goal: _____

😁 Very happy

🙂 Mostly happy

😐 Apathetic

😔 Feeling down

☹️ Sad

😢 Emotional

😭 Distressed/crying

🤢 Sick

Food: _____
_____
_____

What i think prompted this mood: _____
_____
_____

What action can i take for this mood: _____
_____
_____

Something good that happened today: _____
_____

Other Emotions:
Hopeless   Panic attack   Isolated   Lonely   Irritated   Energized   Aggressive   Anger   Other:

Today I am grateful for: _____

Date: _____ Goal for today: _____

MORNING MOOD

Hours Slept: 🌙

Energy Level: 🔋

- 😄 Very happy
- 🙂 Mostly happy
- 😐 Apathetic
- 😔 Feeling down
- 🙁 Sad
- 😢 Emotional
- 😭 Distressed/crying
- 😷 Sick

Other Emotions:
Hopeless   Panic attack   Isolated   Lonely   Irritated   Energized   Aggressive   Anger   Other:

Food: _____
_____
_____

What I think prompted this mood: _____
_____
_____

What action can I take for this mood: _____
_____
_____

Physical Activity today: _____
_____

• •

EVENING MOOD

Progress towards today's goal: _____

- 😄 Very happy
- 🙂 Mostly happy
- 😐 Apathetic
- 😔 Feeling down
- 🙁 Sad
- 😢 Emotional
- 😭 Distressed/crying
- 😷 Sick

Other Emotions:
Hopeless   Panic attack   Isolated   Lonely   Irritated   Energized   Aggressive   Anger   Other:

Food: _____
_____
_____

What I think prompted this mood: _____
_____
_____

What action can I take for this mood: _____
_____
_____

Something good that happened today: _____
_____

Today I am grateful for: _____

Date: _____ Goal for today: _____

MORNING MOOD

Hours Slept: 🌙

Energy Level: 🔋

Food: _____
_____
_____

- 😁 Very happy
- 🙂 Mostly happy
- 😐 Apathetic
- 😔 Feeling down
- 🙁 Sad
- 😢 Emotional
- 🏚 Distressed/crying
- 😷 Sick

What i think prompted this mood: _____
_____
_____

What action can i take for this mood: _____
_____
_____

Physical Activity today: _____
_____

Other Emotions:

Hopeless Panic attack Isolated Lonely Irritated Energized Aggressive Anger Other:

• •

EVENING MOOD

Progress towards today's goal: _____

Food: _____
_____
_____

- 😁 Very happy
- 🙂 Mostly happy
- 😐 Apathetic
- 😔 Feeling down
- 🙁 Sad
- 😢 Emotional
- 🏚 Distressed/crying
- 😷 Sick

What i think prompted this mood: _____
_____
_____

What action can i take for this mood: _____
_____

Something good that happened today: _____
_____

Other Emotions:

Hopeless Panic attack Isolated Lonely Irritated Energized Aggressive Anger Other:

Today I am grateful for: _____

Date: _____ Goal for today: _____

MORNING MOOD

Hours Slept:

Energy Level:

- 😁 Very happy
- 🙂 Mostly happy
- 😐 Apathetic
- 😔 Feeling down
- 🙁 Sad
- 😢 Emotional
- 😭 Distressed/crying
- 😷 Sick

Food: _____
_____
_____

What I think prompted this mood: _____
_____
_____

What action can I take for this mood: _____
_____
_____

Physical Activity today: _____
_____

Other Emotions:
Hopeless   Panic attack   Isolated   Lonely   Irritated   Energized   Aggressive   Anger   Other:

EVENING MOOD

Progress towards today's goal: _____

- 😁 Very happy
- 🙂 Mostly happy
- 😐 Apathetic
- 😔 Feeling down
- 🙁 Sad
- 😢 Emotional
- 😭 Distressed/crying
- 😷 Sick

Food: _____
_____
_____

What I think prompted this mood: _____
_____
_____

What action can I take for this mood: _____
_____
_____

Something good that happened today: _____
_____

Other Emotions:
Hopeless   Panic attack   Isolated   Lonely   Irritated   Energized   Aggressive   Anger   Other:

Today I am grateful for: _____

Date: _____ Goal for today: _____

MORNING MOOD

Hours Slept: 🌙 Energy Level: 🔋

Food: _____

- 😁 Very happy
- 🙂 Mostly happy
- 😐 Apathetic
- 😔 Feeling down
- ☹️ Sad
- 😢 Emotional
- 😭 Distressed/crying
- 😷 Sick

What i think prompted this mood: _____
_____
_____

What action can i take for this mood: _____
_____
_____

Physical Activity today: _____

Other Emotions:
Hopeless   Panic attack   Isolated   Lonely   Irritated   Energized   Aggressive   Anger   Other: _____

• •

EVENING MOOD

Progress towards today's goal: _____

Food: _____

- 😁 Very happy
- 🙂 Mostly happy
- 😐 Apathetic
- 😔 Feeling down
- ☹️ Sad
- 😢 Emotional
- 😭 Distressed/crying
- 😷 Sick

What i think prompted this mood: _____
_____
_____

What action can i take for this mood: _____
_____

Something good that happened today: _____

Other Emotions:
Hopeless   Panic attack   Isolated   Lonely   Irritated   Energized   Aggressive   Anger   Other: _____

Today I am grateful for: _____

Date: _____ Goal for today: _____

MORNING MOOD

Hours Slept: 🌙

Energy Level: 🔋

- 😁 Very happy
- 🙂 Mostly happy
- 😐 Apathetic
- 😞 Feeling down
- 🙁 Sad
- 😢 Emotional
- 😭 Distressed/crying
- 😷 Sick

Food: _____

_____

_____

What i think prompted this mood: _____

_____

_____

What action can i take for this mood: _____

_____

_____

Physical Activity today: _____

_____

Other Emotions:

Hopeless Panic attack Isolated Lonely Irritated Energized Aggressive Anger Other:

• •

EVENING MOOD

Progress towards today's goal: _____

- 😁 Very happy
- 🙂 Mostly happy
- 😐 Apathetic
- 😞 Feeling down
- 🙁 Sad
- 😢 Emotional
- 😭 Distressed/crying
- 😷 Sick

Food: _____

_____

_____

What i think prompted this mood: _____

_____

_____

What action can i take for this mood: _____

_____

Something good that happened today: _____

_____

Other Emotions:

Hopeless Panic attack Isolated Lonely Irritated Energized Aggressive Anger Other:

Today I am grateful for: _____

Congrats!

You tracked your mood for 3 months!

Notes/Observations: _____

_____

_____

_____

_____

_____

_____

_____

_____

_____

_____

_____

_____

_____

_____

_____

_____

_____

_____

_____

_____

_____

_____

_____

_____

Made in the USA
Coppell, TX
26 September 2022

83641679R00056